NEVER LOSE HOPE

NEVER LOSE HOPE

Frazer Discipleship

What is Frazer 365?

Frazer 365 is one church's attempt to touch every member every day with the Word of God. Acts 2:46 teaches that the early church met **"day by day, attending the temple together."** While most members cannot get to our campus every day, we can still study His Word daily together in community. We believe that God works in miraculous ways when every member studies the same Scripture each day. We have also discovered that an expositional approach to the study of Scripture keeps us from skipping the difficult sections and provides us the whole counsel of God's Word.

At Frazer, we believe that the Word of God **"is living and active."** (Hebrews 4:12a)

The Bible is alive with God's truth, and it activates our spiritual growth. Proper application to our daily lives works to help us follow His will.

At Frazer, we believe that the Word of God is **"sharper than any two-edged sword, piercing to the division of soul and of spirit, of joints and of marrow."** (Hebrews 4:12b)

The Bible properly divided, penetrates our lives, and reveals the core of who we are meant to be in Christ. Scripture clearly cuts to the heart of God's purpose and plan for the life He has given us. At times, it painfully points out the sin in our lives.

At Frazer, we believe that the Word of God discerns **"the thoughts and intentions of the heart."** (Hebrews 4:12c)

The Holy Spirit speaks to us through God's Word and uncovers our thoughts and intentions. Scripture points out wrong thinking and misdirected motives and guides us back to a godly mindset, unselfish attitude, and a serving spirit.

At Frazer, we believe that: **"All Scripture is breathed out by God and profitable for teaching, for reproof, for correction, and for training in righteousness, that the man of God may be complete, equipped for every good work."** (2 Timothy 3:16-17)

At Frazer, we believe that His Word is **"a lamp to my feet."** (Psalm 119:105a)

Godly Wisdom comes from His Word. Scripture shines a light on God's will so you can see where He wants your next steps to be.

At Frazer, we believe that His Word is **"a light to my path."** (Psalm 119:105b)

As you commit to **Frazer 365**, may His Word illuminate your path as you take daily steps of faith in your journey with Him.

Never Lose Hope

Hope is future-oriented faith.
John Crotts[1]

The greatest enemy of man is not disease – it's despair.
Anonymous[2]

[4] For whatever was written in former days was written for our instruction, that through endurance and through the encouragement of the Scriptures we might have hope.
the Holy One of Israel, your Savior.
Matthew 15:4 (ESV)

[13] May the God of hope fill you with all joy and peace in believing, so that by the power of the Holy Spirit you may abound in hope.
Matthew 15:13 (ESV)

Table of Contents

Never Lose Hope

Hope is the inextinguishable flicker
God ignites in our souls to keep us believing
in the prevailing power of His light
even when we are surrounded by utter darkness.
Lee Strobel[1]

Introduction

In 1 Corinthians 13:13, Paul named the three essential traits of the Christian life as faith, hope, and love. The Apostle even told us the greatest of these is love. So love is supreme, and faith is the substance. But hope is the least talked about and most misunderstood.

In our culture, hope doesn't mean what it meant in biblical times. Our definition of hope is: maybe something good will happen. When we use the word hope in a sentence, you could replace it with "might." However, biblical hope is a certain expectation of a future reality. When people in Scripture spoke of this word, it was not a "hope-so" talk, but a "know-so" truth.

Maybe a parable about hope will help us as we start our journey. Imagine having a perfect father. I know it is a stretch, but use your holy imagination for this parable and picture a father who always made the right decision with the proper attitude. You never saw him make one mistake in your life. He treated everyone at every time with their best interest at heart. Every time you ever saw him get angry, it was justified and dignified.

Imagine that your father was there for every single significant moment in your life. He never missed a sporting event, awards banquet, or musical recital. He was at home every time you walked in the door. He was continuously there for you and never seemed rushed when you needed to talk. He listened with the greatest heart, and when he spoke, his words always brought the exact wisdom you needed to hear.

At the top of all the other perfect character traits was the most important one: Your father never broke a promise. Imagine you counted the promises your father made, and they numbered over 7,000. And he never broke a single one. He was a promise-making, promise-keeping father.

Your father told you one day about your inheritance. It was another promise he made to you. Your father said that you would live with him in a perfect place one day for all eternity. He promised that, while you would have struggles in your earthly life, you would ultimately be victorious and reign with him forever.

Imagine, after knowing this about your father, that one day he asked you to put all your hope in him. How would you respond knowing your father is perfect and has never let you down? How would you answer knowing your dad has never broken a promise? Could you give one good reason why you wouldn't put your hope in him? You would have every reason for hope because of who your daddy is. You cannot lose because you are certain that no matter what happens in this life, you will live victoriously with your father forever. With that kind of relationship and knowledge of your father, nothing on this side of Heaven could steal your hope.

Now a parable is a short symbolic story told to illustrate a truth or principle. The parable you just read is nothing but the truth about our Heavenly Father that demonstrates our many reasons for always living with hope. May the next five weeks teach you about biblical hope so that you learn to live with certainty in Christ and *Never Lose Hope*.

Day One

Hope

The God of Hope

There is always hope because God is the God of hope.
Anonymous

Text: Romans 15:13
[13] May the God of hope fill you with all joy and peace in believing, so that by the power of the Holy Spirit you may abound in hope.

Thoughts:

We have a Bible full of hope which describes our Father as the God of hope. Lee Strobel details the scriptural concept of hope in Scripture with these words:

> The Bible is a book brimming with hope. All told, there are ninety-seven uses of the word *hope* in the Old Testament and another eighty-three in the New Testament. The theme of hope is woven throughout Scripture. God offers hope so powerful that it can transform a person's life and rewrite a person's future.[1]

As we noted in the introduction, biblical hope is not the same concept of hope that our culture uses. When our society uses the term *hope*, it usually falls under the categories of wishful thinking or possible outcomes. The first refers to positive thinking in an attempt to wish something into existence. Hope means if they stay positive, maybe what they are hoping for will happen. But we all know that, while positive thinking impacts attitude, it doesn't have the power to change the outcome. The second worldly category of hope is dreaming of something while trying to work to make that dream happen. However, just because you earnestly believe in a dream does not guarantee that it will ever become a reality.

In contrast, Lee Strobel provides this great definition of biblical hope:

> Biblical hope is the confident expectation that God is willing and able to fulfill the promises He has made to those who trust in Him.[2]

So, while most people speak of hope as something they do, Scripture describes hope as something believers can have. Christians can have real hope through a relationship with the God of hope.

These truths about biblical hope can be discovered through Paul's writing to the church in Rome. After speaking in chapter 14 about issues that divide strong and weak Christians, Paul writes about what should unite them in 15:1-12. Then, in verse 13, he gives this summary statement as a blessing:

> May the God of hope fill you with all joy and peace in believing, so that by the power of the Holy Spirit you may abound in hope.

This statement connects Paul's next section where the apostle shows how God always planned to extend His message to the Gentile nations. Thus, Paul's words in Romans 15:13 provide a powerful link between a discussion on

Christian relationships and God's desire to bring all nations to faith in Christ. So, the God of hope is the only one who can lead you to abound in hope. The God of hope, through the faith of the believer and the power of the Holy Spirit, can unite all believers with joy and peace.

Paul describes God as the source of all hope, and James Montgomery Boice's commentary unpacks this idea further:

> Without God, our condition is thoroughly, unmistakably, and unalterably hope*less*. We are indeed "without hope and without God in the world" (Eph. 2:12). However, as soon as we bring God into the picture, the situation is reversed. Now we have hope through the work of Jesus Christ, because God Himself is our hope and has given hope to us.
>
> Nothing or no one else can do that. If you put your hope in other people, they will let you down. If you trust your stocks or bank accounts, you will find that they can disappear overnight. Health will fail. Houses can burn. Jobs can be lost. Even great nations enter periods of economic and moral decline. But the one who has his or her hope from the Lord and trusts God as He has revealed Himself in Jesus Christ can stand firm in anything. Edward Mote expressed it in one of our best-known hymns:
>
>> My hope is built on nothing less
>> Than Jesus' blood and righteousness;
>> I dare not trust the sweetest frame,
>> But wholly lean on Jesus' name.
>> On Christ, the solid Rock, I stand;
>> All other ground is sinking sand.
>> His oath, His covenant, His blood
>> Support me in the whelming flood;

When all around my soul gives away,
He then is all my Hope and Stay.
On Christ, the solid Rock, I stand;
All other ground is sinking sand.[3]

Believers can abound in hope through a personal relationship with God who is the fountain from which all hope both flows and flourishes.

Questions:

1. How does biblical hope differ from the world's concept of hope?

2. Why is a believer's ultimate source of hope also his greatest reason for hope?

3. How does abounding hope lead to Christian unity?

4. If you were honest with yourself, would you say that you are currently abounding in hope or lacking in hope? Why do you think this is?

Day Two

Hope

His Promises Provide Hope

When God promises, He is not saying, "I'll try."
He means, "I can, and I will."
James MacDonald[1]

Text: Jeremiah 29:11
[11] For I know the plans I have for you, declares the Lord, plans for welfare and not for evil, to give you a future and a hope.

Thoughts:
Conservative figures reveal that the Bible contains over 7,000 promises. That is a lot of promises considering that all of Scripture consists of 31,173 verses. If studies are correct, that averages out to one promise for every five verses of Scripture. All that clearly shows that we have a God who makes and keeps His promises.

Jeremiah 29:11 contains a promise to the Jews that comes at a horrific time in their history. Jeremiah has just told God's people that they will be carried into exile under Babylonian control and that they will be there for at least 70 years. So God gives them a promise that they have a future after their hardship because He has great plans in store for them. Even through their difficulties, the Jews could maintain their confident expectation in God's plans for their good. And God kept

His promise to Israel. Over seventy years later, Zerubbabel, the grandson of Jehoiachin, led Israel back to their promised land to rebuild the temple (Ezra 1:2-3).

Jeremiah 29:11 is just one example of how God's promises provided hope to God's people. Max Lucado shares how many other heroes of our faith found hope in God's promises:

> The heroes in the Bible came from all walks of life: rulers, servants, teachers, and doctors. They were male, female, single, and married. Yet one common denominator united them: they built their lives on the promises of God. Because of God's promises, Noah believed in rain before *rain* was a word. Because of God's promises, Abraham left a good home for one he'd never seen. Because of God's promises, Joshua led two million people into enemy territory. Because of God's promises, David conked a giant, Peter rose from the ashes of regret, and Paul found a grace worth dying for.
>
> One writer went so far as to call such saints "heirs of the promise" (Hebrews 6:17). It is as if the promise was the family fortune, and they were smart enough to attend the reading of the will.[1]

These words are great reminders that our hope is founded on and continues to flourish because of the promises of God. Peter connects this same truth in his second letter.

2 Peter 1:3-4 (ESV)

[3] His divine power has granted to us all things that pertain to life and godliness, through the knowledge of him who called us to his own glory and excellence, [4] by which he has granted to us his precious and very great promises, so that

through them you may become partakers of the divine nature, having escaped from the corruption that is in the world because of sinful desire.

As believers, God grants us the ability to "become partakers of the divine nature." One of the many character traits of the divine nature is hope (1 Corinthians 13:13). Notice in 2 Peter 1:4, where Peter writes, "so that through them, you become partakers of the divine nature." What exactly is the "them" to which Peter is referring? The "them" is the precious and very great promises that God has given to us. Therefore, 2 Peter 1:3-4 teaches that we are enabled to possess godly traits like hope through the promises God has given us.

When we are tempted to succumb to doubt and despair, we can find reassurance in the promises of His unfailing love and unending grace. As the deported Jews derived hope from Jeremiah 29:11, we too are blessed with divine hope as we focus on God's perfect record in keeping His promises.

Questions:
1. God divinely empowers His followers with the ability to partake in the spiritual nature. In what ways are you living from God's resources through the divine nature? In what ways are you living in the flesh and not realizing your full potential in Christ?

2. How can God's unfailing promises bring more hope into your life?

3. As "heirs of the promise" (Hebrews 6:17), what does Max Lucado's statement from today's devotion mean to you?

It is as if the promise was the family fortune, and they were smart enough to attend the reading of the will.

Day Three

Hope

Hope in His Word

The vigor of our spiritual life will be in exact proportion
to the place held by the Bible in our life and thoughts.
George Muller[1]

Text: Psalm 119:74, 105, 114
[74] Those who fear you shall see me and rejoice, because I have
hoped in your word. . . [105] Your Word is a lamp to my feet and a
light to my path. . . [114] You are my hiding place and my shield; I
hope in your word.

Thoughts:
　　Thus far, we have been reminded that we have a God of
hope who can cause us to abound with hope (Romans 15:13).
We also know that God's promises, and His perfect record of
keeping them, give us reason to have confidence in our future
and allow us to partake of the divine nature (2 Peter 1:3-4).
Today, we focus on the hope found in God's Word.
　　Psalm 119 is known as the Mount Everest of the Psalms because of its 176 verses. This makes it the longest Psalm and the
longest chapter in all of God's Word. Of these 176 verses, all but
five reference the Word of God. So the longest chapter in the Bible focuses solely on the Word of God. More specifically, Psalm
119 highlights the hope we find in God's Word.

In verse 74 the psalmist confesses that he finds hope in God's Word. In verse 114, his hope is so strong in God's Word that he describes God as his hiding place and shield. The Hebrew words for *hope* and *word* are the same in these two verses. *Word* is the Old Testament word *dabar* and it means, "speech, utterances, or words." Therefore, the psalmist's hope comes from the words God speaks and utters to him. The word for *hope* in these two verses is *yachal*. The primary meaning of *yachal* is "to wait expectantly, to cause to hope." When you know God speaks to you, you can have confidence in your relationship with Him. When you hear His voice, you have confidence that He will guide you to future victories.

In between these two verses, the psalmist gives us this hope-filled statement about God's Word: "Your Word is a lamp to my feet and a light to my path." John Phillips explains this description of God's Word as follows:

> "Thy word is a lamp unto my feet, and a light unto my path." A light on the path shows us the direction in which we are heading; a lamp shows us the next step. A light, no matter how bright, will not show us all the twists and turns ahead on the road, but it will give us a general sense of direction. That is what the Bible does. It lights the sinner's path to Christ; it lights the believer's path to glory. "The path of the just is as the shining light that shineth more and more unto the perfect day" (Proverbs 4:18).[2]

When God turns His lamp to shine on your feet, you can take your next step with confidence. When God spotlights your path, you never have to doubt the direction you are headed. Because God knows your future and He lights the way, you can move forward with certainty. His Word gives direction and protection. When you hear Him speak, your hope abounds.

While the Old Testament reveals the hope that comes from God's spoken words, the New Testament extends our hope to His written Word. Notice Paul's words:

Romans 15:4 (ESV)
⁴ For whatever was written in former days was written for our instruction, that through endurance and through the encouragement of the Scriptures we might have hope.

Everything in Scripture was written for the ultimate purpose of bringing hope to our lives. Scripture teaches us about the endurance of others to encourage us to imitate their hope. God has never failed to accomplish His purposes in the past, and He will never fail us in the future. The Bible is full of examples of people who faced extreme difficulties yet still persevered and saw God's promises fulfilled in their lives. So we have a God who speaks to light our way. In addition, we have a God who inspired Scripture full of testimonies so we can read and be reminded of His power and goodness. We have been given everything we need to hope in His Word.

Questions:
1. In what specific ways does God's Word bring you hope?

2. How significant is the message of Romans 15:4 to your journey of hope?

3. How can the following Scriptures help you hope in His Word?

Isaiah 30:21 (ESV)
    ²¹ And your ears shall hear a word behind you, saying, "This is the way, walk in it," when you turn to the right or when you turn to the left.

Psalm 29:3-5 (ESV)
    ³ The voice of the Lord is over the waters; the God of glory thunders, the Lord, over many waters. ⁴ The voice of the Lord is powerful; the voice of the Lord is full of majesty.
    ⁵ The voice of the Lord breaks the cedars; the Lord breaks the cedars of Lebanon.

Day Four

Hope

The Cause for Courage

Courage is like love; it must have hope for nourishment.
Napoleon[1]

Text: Deuteronomy 31:6-8

[6] "Be strong and courageous. Do not fear or be in dread of them, for it is the Lord your God who goes with you. He will not leave you or forsake you." [7] Then Moses summoned Joshua and said to him in the sight of all Israel, "Be strong and courageous, for you shall go with this people into the land that the Lord has sworn to their fathers to give them, and you shall put them in possession of it. [8] It is the Lord who goes before you. He will be with you; He will not leave you or forsake you. Do not fear or be dismayed."

Thoughts:

The phrase "be strong and courageous" is repeated 25 times in the Bible. God speaks these words four times directly to Joshua (Deuteronomy 31:23; Joshua 1:6, 7, 9). At other times, God sends the same message to Joshua through His servant Moses (Deuteronomy 31:6-8). Why does God have to repeat this message so often to an incredible leader like Joshua? Because we all need encouragement and strength to courageously face our fears. As Napoleon once said, "Courage must have hope for nourishment."

However, God doesn't just simply speak the words "be strong and courageous" and expect us to bow our necks and will ourselves to tough it out. Fear is a real emotion and overcoming it does not happen through just positive thinking. Good thing God gave us some incredible reasons not to be afraid.

Our awesome God gives three incredible causes for courage in our Scripture for today. The first reason we can have courage is because God goes before us (Deuteronomy 31:8). When God sends us into a battle, He goes before us to lead the way. Deuteronomy 1:30 declares, "The Lord your God who goes before you will himself fight for you . . . before your eyes." You can be strong and courageous when you know God goes before you.

Not only does God go before you, but He also walks with you (Deuteronomy 31:6 and 8). This is the second cause for courage. The God who leads the way also stays with you all the way. The confidence that comes from knowing God is there - infuses courage into your soul.

The third cause for courage is the following phrase: "He will not leave you or forsake you" (Deuteronomy 31:8). You can go wherever God calls you with courage because He has promised to never leave you. God never abandons His children. So, what else do you need to cause you to live with courage? Put your hope in these truths. God is your Guard and your Guide. He goes before you, He is also right beside you, and He will never leave your side.

One of the many things that I love about God is He doesn't just tell us these truths, but He also illustrates them through the lives of His people. As you study Scripture, you will notice that everything Moses told Joshua about God in Deuteronomy 31:6-8, God later demonstrated personally to Joshua in Joshua 2 and 3. These chapters of Joshua record the miracle crossing of the Jordan River at flood stage, which marked the nation's long-awaited entrance into the Promised Land.

God had directed the priests to take up the ark of the covenant and proceed ahead of His people. The ark of the covenant contained the mercy seat where God's presence resided, so the ark symbolized God's presence going before them to lead the way into the Promised Land. When the priests who were carrying the ark of the covenant stepped into the raging waters of the Jordan River, God parted the river by backing up the water into a heap on both sides so that His people could cross on dry ground.

A very unique instruction is found in Joshua 3:4. The people had to follow the ark of the covenant from a distance of approximately ten football fields. God's presence would go before them, but His power demanded their reverence and respect. Imagine walking behind the priest and watching from a distance, as the rushing water that had flooded the river suddenly stopped and the riverbed miraculously dried up before your eyes. And all of this occurred around the ark of the covenant, which you knew to symbolize God's presence. Just as Moses told the people in Deuteronomy 31:8, "It is the Lord who goes before you."

Then, as the priest holding the ark of the covenant stood in the middle of the Jordan River on dry ground, the entire nation of Israel passed by. The presence of God, pictured by the ark of the covenant, stood between the river and their reward. In between the bank and their blessing was their God. Just as Moses said to Joshua years earlier in Deuteronomy 31:8, "He will be with you."

Then after the entire nation had crossed over the Jordan River, the priest carrying the ark of the covenant walked out on the other side. Joshua 4:18 records what happened next:

> ¹⁸ And when the priests bearing the ark of the covenant of the Lord came up from the midst of the Jordan, and

the soles of the priests' feet were lifted up on dry ground, the waters of the Jordan returned to their place and overflowed all its banks, as before.

Surely God went before them, stood beside them, and even walked behind them as their rear guard. The words of Moses to Joshua in Deuteronomy 31:8 could not have been a better commentary on what occurred in Joshua 3-4. God never left them. He did not forsake them. They did not have to fear or be dismayed because God walked with them each step of the way.

God's presence is more than enough reason for you not to despair. May the knowledge of His continual presence before you, beside you, and behind you, cause you to live courageously for Him.

Questions:

1. Which of the three causes for courage encourages you the most and why?

2. How does God's visual aid with the ark of the covenant and the miracle crossing of the Jordan River give you more confidence in these biblical truths?

3. In your prayer time, focus on God's presence with you and let hope nourish your courage.

Day Five

Hope

What You Need to Know

Hope, from the biblical perspective, is a future certainty
grounded in a present reality.
Victor Shepherd[1]

Text: Ephesians 1:16-23

[16] I do not cease to give thanks for you, remembering you in
my prayers, [17] that the God of our Lord Jesus Christ, the Father
of glory, may give you the Spirit of wisdom and of revelation
in the knowledge of him, [18] having the eyes of your hearts enlightened, that you may know what is the hope to which he has
called you, what are the riches of his glorious inheritance in the
saints, [19] and what is the immeasurable greatness of his power
toward us who believe, according to the working of his great
might [20] that He worked in Christ when he raised him from the
dead and seated him at his right hand in the heavenly places, [21] far above all rule and authority and power and dominion,
and above every name that is named, not only in this age but
also in the one to come. [22] And he put all things under his feet
and gave him as head over all things to the church, [23] which is
His body, the fullness of him who fills all in all.

Thoughts:

Ephesians 1:16-23 contains Paul's powerful prayer for the
believers in Ephesus. He had a genuine concern for God's

people to live a victorious life, and he understood that belief impacts behavior. So Paul prayed that every believer would know three essential things.

First, Paul prayed, "that the God of our Lord Jesus Christ, the Father of glory, may give you the Spirit of wisdom and of revelation in the knowledge of him" (verse 17). Paul was simply praying for believers to know God better. Why is this important? Richard Coekin answers this question:

> Because God is so unutterably captivating in his gracious holiness that knowing Him will be our supreme blessing for eternity. The greatest blessing that anyone can experience is to know God, and to know Him better every day.[2]

Not only do we need to know God better, but we need to know the hope of God's calling on our lives. In verse 18, Paul prayed: ". . . having the eyes of your hearts enlightened, that you may know what is the hope to which he has called you." Coekin gives great insight into this calling:

> God knows that the way we "see" in this world – what we value and desire or fear and avoid – is not just a rational decision based upon information neutrally observed. Our perspectives depend upon our values, which are shaped by the affections of our hearts.
>
> The word "heart" is used in the Bible not to describe the organ pumping blood around our limbs, but the center of our physical and spiritual being, combining our intellectual understanding and our personal affections. So Paul prays that the "eyes of their hearts" will be enlightened by God to love the things that God

loves so that these Christians will see the world the way God does, which is the way it really is.

It is vital to understand that so often in our Christian lives, God doesn't want to alter the circumstances of our lives but to alter the way we see those circumstances, by changing our hearts. For example, the apostle is suffering in prison, but we don't hear him asking for prayer to be released, but for courage to "make known the mystery of the gospel, for which I am an ambassador in chains" (Ephesians 6:19–20). Those around him who do not know God or understand the gospel might see him as a defeated preacher, trapped in the misery of a Roman dungeon. But with the eyes of his heart enlightened by the eternal plans of God, Paul sees himself as a dignified ambassador of Christ, gathering others under the rule of Christ, with a wonderful opportunity to evangelize his fellow prisoners and guards, and so to demonstrate in the heavenly realms that Christ is enthroned in victory over his enemies. That is quite a shift of perspective![3]

We need God to open the eyes of our hearts so that we can see things from His perspective. We desperately need to know the hope of His calling. When that happens, we are infused with a stronger desire to fulfill His purpose.

Paul closes out his prayer with a focus on knowing God's power (Ephesians 1:19-23). God's power is unparalleled and already demonstrated. We know He has the power to raise us because He has already raised Jesus from the dead. We also know that God fills us with His incredible power.

So pray this prayer for yourself and other believers. Ask God to help you understand what we all need to know. First, know Him better. Second, know why He called you and what He has called you to. And third, know that God will fill you with His power to accomplish His purpose for your life. When you know all of that, you can live with a confident hope in God.

Questions:

1. How can a deepening knowledge of God, His calling, and His power impact your prayer life? Is there anything you can take away from today's devotion and start applying in your prayers?

2. The word "knowledge" in verse 17 means "a full discernment" or "a perceptive recognition." What could full discernment or a perceptive recognition of God look like in your relationship with Him?

3. Paul uses a different word for "know" in verse 18. It is the Greek word *oida* that means, "to see with physical eyes." It can also mean to "mentally see." God wants you to mentally see the hope of His calling. How can you envision what God has called you to and how does this mentality give you hope?

Day Six

Hope

God Always Finishes What He Starts

God hasn't brought you this far
and forgotten your name.
Bob Goff[1]

Text: Philippians 1:6
[6] And I am sure of this, that he who began a good work in you will bring it to completion at the day of Jesus Christ.

Thoughts:

An uncertain future can lead to a sense of hopelessness. Charles Swindoll tells the following story that illustrates this reality:

Years ago an S-4 submarine was rammed by a ship off the coast of Massachusetts. It sank immediately. The entire crew was trapped in a prison house of death. Every effort was made to rescue the crew, but all ultimately failed. Near the end of the ordeal, a deep-sea diver, who was doing everything in his power to find a way for the crew's release, thought he heard a tapping on the steel wall of the sunken sub. He placed his helmet up against the side of the vessel and realized that the sound he heard was Morse Code. He attached himself to the side of the sub and spelled out in his mind the message being tapped from within. It was repeating the same question. The question was, from within: "Is - there - any - hope?"[2]

That is the same question that many people are asking within their own hearts. Is there any hope for a happy ending? Is there any hope that things are going to work out? What happens when life ends here on this earth? Is there any hope?

As believers, we know the answer to that question. Yes, there is always hope with Jesus because we are fully confident that God always finishes what He starts. Paul wrote these words with profound certainty: "And I am sure of this, that he who began a good work in you will bring it to completion at the day of Jesus Christ" (Philippians 1:6). When Paul wrote these words, he was imprisoned for preaching the Gospel of Christ. Paul did not allow his poor worldly situations to negatively impact his spiritual expectations. He was sure that God started a good work in him and that He would carry it to completion.

David Jeremiah, in his book *Hope: Living Fearlessly in a Scary World*, says:

> Biblical hope is not wishful thinking. It's not a lucky chance. It's not ungrounded optimism. No, it's a rock-solid belief in the character of God. That's not to say we are guaranteed rosebushes without thorns or a life free from tragedy or disaster. But because we know that God is all-knowing and all-powerful and for us, we can face down our fears and trust the outcome of our circumstances to Him.[3]

Maxie Dunnam adds this wisdom on Philippians 1:6:

> Remember: God did not start His work within us to abandon it. He does not do things half-measure. We have

24

the promise: He will complete what He started. Let us claim that promise and come to Him again in faith, in the same yieldedness as when we first gave our life to Him.

What the Christian can count on is a God who keeps faith. The truth of Philippians 1:6 runs throughout Paul's theological stance. He persistently insists, "God is faithful" (1 Corinthians 1:9; 10:30; 2 Corinthians 1:18; 1 Thessalonians 5:24). Because God is faithful and is going to complete what He started within us, we can appropriate the cross-resurrection way of life. We can "go on to completion" because God has already invested his total self in us. We can face the coming judgment without fear for our relationship with God has been made right through Christ; we can expect the Christian mission to be fully and finally accomplished.[4]

The hope for our future comes from the trust we have in a God who is always faithful. That confidence originates from our personal relationship with God that started by faith. Our hope continues to grow stronger every day because we know that no matter what happens in this life, God always finishes what He starts.

Questions:
1. How does the character of God contribute to your faith?

2. How does the continual growth of your faith impact your hope?

3. How does Paul's situation surrounding the writing of Philippians challenge you to keep the right perspective?

Day Seven

Hope

What Pleases God

What delights the heart of God and brings a smile to His face are people who revere His name and place their total confidence in His steadfast love.
Jonathan Munson[1]

Text: Psalm 147:7-11
[7] Sing to the Lord with thanksgiving; make melody to our God on the lyre! [8] He covers the heavens with clouds; he prepares rain for the earth; he makes grass grow on the hills. [9] He gives to the beasts their food, and to the young ravens that cry. [10] His delight is not in the strength of the horse, nor his pleasure in the legs of a man, [11] but the Lord takes pleasure in those who fear him, in those who hope in his steadfast love.

Thoughts:
God is our perfect Heavenly Father. As such, there are certain things about His children that please Him. The Psalmist gives us two specific things that God delights in: "those who fear him" and "those who hope in his steadfast love" (Psalm 147:11).

First, it pleases God when we fear Him. When we fear God, it shows that we recognize He is God. When we revere God, we will surrender to His mighty power and trust His Lordship over our lives. God knows that if we rightfully fear Him, we will obey

27

all His commands. God knows we can live under His perfect will for our lives as long as we follow His Word. So He delights to see His children living out what He has purposed and planned.

Every parent knows this on an imperfect and lesser scale. We have plans and desires for our kids. When they listen to us, we can protect them and guide them to succeed in life. When they disobey us, they suffer the consequences that we were trying to protect them from. Yet we are imperfect parents with limited knowledge. We don't know with certainty what's going to happen or what all God has planned for our children's lives.

God is the flawless Father, and He has perfect plans. He is also all-knowing and all-powerful, so God knows in advance what we could be if we follow His will. Everything about our future spiritual growth hinges on our obedience to His commands. Our obedience hinges, in part, on how much we fear God. Although it should not be the only motivator, Scripture repeatedly demonstrates that we cannot set it aside. One of Solomon's best-known proverbs boldly declares that "The fear of the Lord is the beginning of wisdom" (Proverbs 9:10). In Deuteronomy 10:12-13, 20-21a, Moses says, "What does the Lord your God require of you, but to fear the Lord your God, to walk in all his ways, to love him, to serve the Lord your God with all your heart and with all your soul, to keep the commandments and statutes of the Lord, which I am commanding you today for your good . . . You shall fear the Lord your God. You shall serve him and hold fast to him, and by his name you shall swear. He is your praise. He is your God."

In this Scripture, we see both fear of the Lord and love of the Lord joined together. This is because God's delight in us doesn't just come when we fear Him. God is fully pleased when we expect his love for us and then love him in return.

Yet God's delight in us doesn't just come when we fear Him. God is fully pleased when we expect His love for us. That's why the psalmist said, "The Lord takes pleasure . . . in those who hope in his steadfast love." The Living Bible paraphrases the end of verse 11 as follows: "But His joy is in those who expect Him to be loving and kind."

How important is it to you that your children know that you love them? As a parent, I want my children to have complete assurance that I love them. When they have complete confidence in my love for them, they have no reason to doubt the motives behind what I tell them. So when they are tempted to rebel against my authority, I want them to know I am giving them direction because I love them. It brings me incredible joy when my children do what I say because they trust in how much I love them.

What God says to us comes out of His unbelievable love for us. We will be much more likely to consistently obey God when we realize how steadfast His great love is for us. Imagine how much joy our Heavenly Father feels when we completely trust His steadfast love.

Questions:
1. Has reading today's devotion changed your perspective about fearing God? In what ways?

2. How is your hope in God's steadfast love based on His past goodness and your future expectation of His unchanging love?

3. What are your thoughts on the following quote by J.C. Ryle?

Christ's love towards us, and not our love towards Christ, is the true ground of expectation, and the true foundation of hope.[2]

Day Eight

Hope

Born Again into a Living Hope

The character of the hope is in the word "living."
This hope is not past tense. It has not expired.
It is a hope that is alive.
John G. Butler[1]

Text: 1 Peter 1:3-5
[3] Blessed be the God and Father of our Lord Jesus Christ!
According to his great mercy, He has caused us to be born
again to a living hope through the resurrection of Jesus Christ
from the dead,[4] to an inheritance that is imperishable, unde-
filed, and unfading, kept in heaven for you, [5] who by God's
power are being guarded through faith for a salvation ready
to be revealed in the last time.

Thoughts:
　　What words first come to mind when you think about the
subject of salvation? If you grew up going to church, these
three expressions would have to be at the top of your list:
faith, grace, and born again. We know that we are saved by
our faith through God's grace (Ephesians 2:8). Jesus Himself
connected salvation with the term "born again" in His con-
versation with Nicodemus in John 3:3. In our Scripture for
today, Peter says that God has caused us to be born again to
a living hope (1 Peter 1:3). Have you ever thought about the

word "hope" in reference to your salvation?

Most definitions of hope contain a futuristic focus. We say, "I hope that it doesn't rain next week." Most people only connect their concept of hope with future events. However, Scripture teaches us that hope is also a great salvation word.

Notice several things about Peter's statement in 1 Peter 1:3. First, "God causes us to be born again." "Born again" reminds us that there are two births. At your physical birth, you were simply born. At your spiritual birth, you were born again. When you were born for the first time, you instantly became children of your parents. When you were born again, you immediately became a child of God. The "again" adds significant weight to the second birth. What does "again" mean? At my salvation, something occurred again, similar to what happened at my physical birth. As my body came alive at conception, my spirit came alive at conversion. My earthly parents caused my first birth, but God caused the second one.

Observe how Peter continues his statement: "God has caused us to be born again to a living hope." When God gave us a new birth, it came with a living hope. This is better understood by contrasting a lost and saved person's hope. Lost people only have hope that falls into the category of "future wishful thinking." Since they have only had one birth, a physical one, their hope remains in the physical realm. Since saved people have had a second birth, a spiritual one, they have a spiritual dimension of hope. Therefore, saved people have a hope that contains confident expectations concerning the future and a present-tense reality. First, the future hope of a believer far surpasses the wishful thinking that occurs in the physical realm. Believers have a future hope that is based on the certainty of God's promises and the assurance of God's character. Second, a Christian has a far more powerful hope that comes through salvation. Because Jesus rose from the dead and is seated on the throne, believers live with a current hope that empowers them as they head toward their certain future.

That is why we are born again into a "living" hope. As Christians, our hope is not just for one day. That same hope lives in us every day. Hope came to life the same millisecond our spirit was brought to life – the moment you were saved. Because of your salvation, your hope lives on a firm foundation. Because it is a living hope, it lives every day through the same power that raised Jesus from the dead. Your hope can thrive daily because your future inheritance is secure.

Living daily with a living hope is a character trait of the people of God. So, while we look to the future and eternal life, we are filled with hope that transcends any circumstances of this life. And nothing can extinguish a living hope that was birthed the day you got saved. "God has caused us to be born again to a living hope." Our hope is living only because Jesus is alive and "death no longer has dominion over him" (Romans 6:9). May that powerful hope continually grow more and more each day so everyone you meet will know that it is alive and well.

Questions:
1. What does "born again" mean to you?

2. How does the word "hope" go perfectly with the term "salvation"?

3. In what ways does your life reveal that your hope is alive?

Hope

The Anchor for Our Soul

For a drifting ship, the anchor plunges down from the deck
into black waters below. The Lord Jesus Christ, though, is an
anchor extending up into Heaven. As you wait for the day when
your faith becomes sight, you have hope.
John Crotts[1]

Text: Hebrews 6:17-20

[17] So when God desired to show more convincingly to the
heirs of the promise the unchangeable character of his purpose, he guaranteed it with an oath, [18] so that by two unchangeable things, in which it is impossible for God to lie, we
who have fled for refuge might have strong encouragement
to hold fast to the hope set before us. [19] We have this as a sure
and steadfast anchor of the soul, a hope that enters into the
inner place behind the curtain, [20] where Jesus has gone as a
forerunner on our behalf, having become a high priest forever after the order of Melchizedek.

Thoughts:

Anchors keep boats from drifting with the current. However, one thing I have learned about anchors is that they must be
used properly. You can tie the rope off to your boat, throw your
anchor into the water, and still not stop your boat from drifting.
A heavy anchor can still slide on shifting sand, while a light

anchor can remain immovable if wedged between solid rocks. The power of the anchor's hold is directly related to the foundation upon which that anchor rests.

We live in a world drifting away from God. It's full of evil and wickedness, and a dangerous undercurrent of popular opinion is causing tides to flow against God's Word. The Good News is that, through Christ, we have an anchor for our souls connected to a sure foundation.

According to the writer of Hebrews, this sure foundation consists of two unchangeable components: God's promise and God's oath. Since it is impossible for God to lie, He will never break His promise. And since God could never find a name greater than His to make an oath by, we have the complete assurance that God will fulfill what He promises. God's oath puts His name on the covenant contract. So you can know what God says is signed, sealed, and delivered. In a drifting world, we can anchor our lives into the solid foundation of the promises and character of God.

Hebrews 6:20 goes on to describe how Jesus, as the anchor for our souls, brings us hope. Jesus is our High Priest and goes behind the veil into God's presence to intercede on our behalf. His power, presence, and work on our behalf give us complete certainty in future victory over sin and death. In a world that is constantly changing, we anchor to the God who is the same yesterday, today, and forever (Hebrews 13:8).

Because we have this "sure and steadfast anchor of the soul," the writer of Hebrews says, "hold fast to the hope set before us" (Hebrews 6:18). As an anchor holds firmly to a sure foundation, it is our responsibility to grab hold of God's finished work in Christ with our hands of hope.

As we close out today's reflection on Hebrews 6:19-20, may this teaching from Albert Mohler bring you hope as you hold on to the anchor of your soul:

The author poignantly reminds his people of their need for "an anchor for the soul." The troubles and temptations of this world throw our souls around far too often. And yet, we have a sure and steadfast anchor that stabilizes our souls amidst the waves of this world. The promises of God are firm and secure enough to hold us steady in a storm. God's promise and oath anchor the hope that "enters the inner sanctuary behind the curtain," which is the most holy place.

Once a year, on the Day of Atonement, the high priest went into the most holy place and offered the blood of an animal in order to turn God's wrath away from Israel. Jesus, as our high priest, entered the inner place behind the curtain and offered his own blood on our behalf. Our anchor, Jesus, has gone before us as our forerunner to accomplish all that God's justice requires. As our great high priest, Jesus has purchased our salvation and assured us of the promises of God. Thus, Jesus's atoning work on the cross predicates the Christian's hope and anchors the Christian's soul.[2]

Questions:

1. In what ways do you see our world drifting? In what ways do you struggle with drifting in your own spiritual journey?

2. Why is an anchor a perfect picture of our hope in Jesus?

3. What helps you hold on to what God has set before you?

4. What did you learn from today's lesson about hope?

Hope

Good Hope

It is because God gives His people "good hope"
that He is "the God of hope" (Romans 15:13).
F.F. Bruce[1]

Text: 2 Thessalonians 2:16-17

[16] Now may our Lord Jesus Christ himself, and God our Father, who loved us and gave us eternal comfort and good hope through grace, [17] comfort your hearts and establish them in every good work and word.

Thoughts:

Paul, in his second letter to Thessalonica, says that God has given us "eternal comfort and good hope through grace." We can have never-ending encouragement because, through God's grace, He gives us a hope that is good. To better understand the biblical truths of this good hope, we need a quick study of the New Testament words for "good."

Two different Greek words are translated as "good." One is *agathos*. This word refers to being good in character and carries the idea of being upright and pure. So *agathos* means something is inherently good, and it describes the goodness that originates from God's character. Believers are empowered for godly living through the goodness of God.

Another word for "good" is *kalos*. This word refers to a good outward expression or a noble deed. *Kalos* is sometimes translated as "beautiful." Potters would inscribe *kalos* on their vases

39

next to their names to symbolize that their pottery was attractive and good.

So there are very specific uses for *agathos* and *kalos*. *Agathos* is resisting temptation by living in purity, while *kalos* is providing a homeless man a meal. A person can do *kalos* without having *agathos*. Someone who isn't inherently pure can still do something beautiful for someone else. However, if you truly have *agathos*, it will lead to *kalos*. When you are filled with the goodness of God, your life will be beautiful and attractive to others.

It is very enlightening to see when both of these words show up in the same Scripture. Jesus Himself made a clear distinction between a good character (*agathos*) and a good or beautiful action (*kalos*). Notice the following Scripture and the use of *agathos* and *kalos*.

Matthew 7:17-20 (ESV)

[17] "So, every healthy (*agathos*) tree bears good (*kalos*) fruit, but the diseased tree bears bad fruit. [18] A healthy (*agathos*) tree cannot bear bad fruit, nor can a diseased tree bear good (*kalos*) fruit. [19] Every tree that does not bear good (*kalos*) fruit is cut down and thrown into the fire. [20] Thus you will recognize them by their fruits."

So when the root of our tree is inherently good (*agathos*), the fruit of our lives will be beautiful (*kalos*) to God.

So back to our "good hope" found in 2 Thessalonians 2:16-17. The word Paul uses for good is *agathos*. Our hope is founded on the character and goodness of God. As a believer, you have a hope that is good because God is inherently good. Your hope is as secure as God's goodness is certain.

In verse 17, Paul gives an unbelievable twist on the meaning of *agathos*. After he says that God gave us His good hope, he closes this section of his letter by asking God to "Comfort your hearts and establish them in every good (*agathos*) work and word." Rather than use *kalos* for the good work as Jesus does in Matthew 17, Paul keeps the word *agathos* for good work and word. Paul is making an incredible point. When we have hope that comes from the character and goodness of God, the things we say and do aren't just beautiful, they are established on the righteous goodness of God. That is some GOOD hope!!

Questions:
1. Why do people sometimes put more emphasis on their outward good works than on the internal goodness of their heart?

2. How can beautiful works leave you in a bad situation if your heart isn't spiritually good?

3. What are your thoughts on the importance of *agathos*?

4. How is *agathos* hope not only good but also the best?

Day Eleven

Hope

Faith Is the Foundation for Hope

Faith is looking at God and trusting Him for everything,
while hope is looking at the future and trusting God for it.
Tom Wright[1]

Text: Hebrews 11:1-3
[1] Now faith is the assurance of things hoped for, the conviction of things not seen. [2] For by it the people of old received their commendation. [3] By faith we understand that the universe was created by the word of God, so that what is seen was not made out of things that are visible.

Thoughts:
Faith and hope are both foundational to our relationship with Christ. Peter writes that God revealed Himself through Jesus, raised Him from the dead, and gave Him glory so that our faith and hope would be in God (1 Peter 1:20-21). God wants our faith and hope to be in Him, and knowing Jesus brings us both.

Faith can be defined as personal trust. Hope is often described as our future confidence. The writer of Hebrews connects hope to faith. Tom Wright says:

Faith is always closely linked to hope. As we see in verse 1, Hebrews actually defines faith in relation to hope. It's one thing to have hope, but when you have faith underneath, it assures it. I may hope for a better world, for a new bodily life beyond the grave; but unless I believe in the God who raised Jesus, my hope may degenerate into mere optimism. I may have a general sense that there are unseen realities around me, perhaps even some kind of personal force for good with whom I should have some sort of a relationship; but unless I believe in the God we know in Jesus, this sense of unseen things will lack conviction. [2]

Faith and hope are essential ingredients to our life in Christ. John Piper gives these profound statements regarding faith and hope:

Faith is the experience of the substance of future reality known, believed, tasted, and cherished now. Biblical hope is biblical faith in the future tense. *Christian hope is a confidence that something will come to pass because God has promised it will come to pass.*[3]

Hope is looking expectantly towards the future based on God's faithfulness in the past and our current trust in Him. So biblical hope is founded on our faith. "Faith is the assurance of things hoped for" (Hebrews 11:1). Faith and hope, by definition, complement each other. We cannot have one without the other. Without faith, there is no future hope; without hope, there is no genuine faith.

Since faith is the foundation for hope, faith comes first. Our hope grows from our faith. This means that our hope will never be stronger than our faith. Because we fully believe in God, we have complete hope for a better life.

Once the foundation of faith is laid down in your life, you can begin to hope with confidence that your future is secure.

That is why Hebrews 11:1 says, "Now faith is the assurance of things hoped for, the conviction of things not seen." You can live with strong convictions that God will accomplish things you haven't seen because you live by faith. And that faith gives you the assurance for your hope. Keep the faith so your hope will be strong. Today, live with complete confidence based on your firm faith in Jesus Christ.

Questions:

1. Have you considered before how your faith and hope are connected? What are your thoughts about hope being founded on faith?

2. Based on today's lesson, what is the surest way to keep your hope strong?

3. How does the following verse connect hope to faith?

Romans 15:13 (ESV)
[13] May the God of hope fill you with all joy and peace in believing, so that by the power of the Holy Spirit you may abound in hope.

Day Twelve

Hope

God Is in Control

The antidote to fear is faith.
And faith gives us hope in the midst of whatever we face.
David Jeremiah[1]

Text: 2 Timothy 1:7
[7] for God gave us a spirit not of fear but of power and love and self-control.

Thoughts:
Faith and fear constantly battle against one another. Both are based on our future. Fear robs us of faith, while faith empowers us to overcome our fears. Since fear is the greatest hindrance to our faith, fear is also our greatest barrier to hope.

David Jeremiah expounds on these truths through his comments on 2 Timothy 1:7. He explains how God is the answer to all of our fears so we can live with greater hope. May his words give you great wisdom to apply to your life today:

When the apostle Paul was giving counsel to Timothy, his young protégé, he knew Timothy was afraid of something - probably of his assignment to lead the large church in Ephesus. Timothy was raised in a small town in Asia Minor, and Ephesus was the big city. Paul himself had spent three years in Ephesus, building up the church there. It was led by a strong group of elders, yet false teachers were causing trouble. And Timothy was supposed to go in and be the leader of the whole thing. What young pastor wouldn't have felt fear at the prospect?

So what did Paul tell Timothy? "Your fear is not from God. What comes from God are power, love, and a stable mental attitude" (2 Timothy 1:7, my paraphrase).

Paul knew that when we get God's perspective on the source of our fear, we can set aside what is not from Him and embrace what is. In all my years of following Christ, studying the Bible, and pastoring well-intentioned Christians, I have yet to find a fear for which God does not have an answer. And the reason is simple: God Himself is the answer to all our fears.

Think about it—fear is almost always based on the future. Whether the future is just a minute from now (you're waiting on a doctor's diagnosis) or five years from now (you worry about having enough money for retirement), fear's home office is the future.

But what is the future to God? To Him, the future is now! We live inside time while God, who made it, lives outside it. We know relatively little about the future, while God knows everything about it. All the events in our lives occur in two time frames: past and future. (The present is a continuously fleeing, infinitesimal moment that becomes past even before we can define it.) God, on the other hand, has only one frame of reference: the eternal now, in which He sees and knows everything, including the future.

That's why God is the answer to all our fears. If God is good and loving (and He is), and if God is all-powerful (and He is), and if God has a purpose and a plan that includes His children (and He does), and if we are His children (as I hope you are), then there is no reason to fear and every reason to hope, for God is in control of everything.

I know that's good theology, and you probably believe it. But you still have fears and apprehensions and a hollow place in the pit of your stomach, either sometimes or all the time. It's one thing to know something with the mind, and another to believe it with the heart.

How do you help a little child face her fear of the darkness? First, you appeal to the mind. You turn on the light and show her there's nothing scary in the room. Then you help her attune her heart to what her mind has accepted. This is the process of faith, for all of us. We accept that God is in control, and on that basis, we shift our burdens to His perfect shoulders.

But what about our shaky future? Pessimism doesn't work because it's another form of mental enslavement. Optimism may have no basis in reality. The one way to walk with hope and confidence into an unknown future is to stake everything on the power, goodness, and faithfulness of God.

To understand why God is the answer to all our fears, we must understand what the Bible says about fear. And it says a lot. It tells us more than three hundred times not to fear. "Fear not" is its most frequently repeated command. The word afraid occurs more than two hundred times, and fear more than four hundred. And lest you think our Bible heroes were fearless, more than two hundred individuals in Scripture are said to have been afraid. And not all these were the "bad guys"; many were the main characters - David, Paul, Timothy, and others.

Biblical heroes were regular people who had to learn the same things you and I have to learn - to drive out fear by increasing their knowledge of God, to shift their focus from their present fear to their eternal hope, to replace what they didn't know about the future with what they did know about Him. They had to put away childish things (being afraid of everything) and grow up in their faith and understanding.[2]

I know that was a lot of outside discussion quoted from Dr. David Jeremiah. However, sometimes it is impossible to say it better than it has already been said. May God grant you more faith in Him and less fear about your future as you live with the confidence that God is in control.

Questions:
1. How can knowing that God is outside of time and already knows the future help you combat the attacks of fear?

2 Why is it essential to know that God has given you a spirit of power, love, and self-control? How do each of these three elements strengthen your faith to conquer your fears?

3. Dr. Jeremiah describes faith as a process in which we move from knowing something true about God with our minds to believing that truth with our hearts and then trusting God with our burdens. Reflect on the burdens and fears that you face and – in an attitude of prayer – take some time to apply truth to those fears.

Day Thirteen

Hope

God's Love Fuels Our Hope

⁵ and hope does not put us to shame,
because God's love has been poured into our hearts
through the Holy Spirit who has been given to us.
Romans 5:5 (ESV)

Text: 1 Corinthians 13:13
¹³ So now faith, hope, and love abide, but the greatest of these is love.

Thoughts:
God has given us three major virtues to live out a spiritually abundant life. These three great gifts are faith, hope, and love. In the previous two days, we have studied the unique connection between faith and hope. Both of these are also connected to our greatest virtue, which is love.

Paul teaches us in Romans 5:5 that God has poured out the love we need into our hearts through the Holy Spirit. R. Kent Hughes describes it as follows:

> The idea in Greek is that God's love has been and continues to be poured out within our hearts. This is a picture of unstinting lavishness. Our hearts have been filled to overflowing with divine affection. The agent of this is the Holy Spirit, who personally

represents God's love in our hearts.[1]

God ensures we have His love filling our hearts. He gives us His love because He knows that is our greatest need. Our faith grows best when we are full of His love. And God's love is the fuel that ignites and sustains our hope.

For a moment today, imagine attempting to put your faith in God without His love. How hard would it be to trust in God if you didn't know He loved you? How difficult would it be to place all your hope in someone who doesn't love you? Our faith and hope are vitally connected to God's love for us.

Did you know that what sets Christianity apart is the resurrection of Jesus and the love of God? Christianity is unique in that all other belief systems follow a dead prophet or founder. In addition, all other religions are based on serving someone who is distant and uncaring. There is no hope for eternity without the resurrection and no growing relationship with God without knowing that He loves you.

When you understand the depths of God's love for you, it gives you a greater desire to put your faith and hope in Him. He loves you more than anyone else ever could, and He wants what's best for you. His purpose for your life is backed by His love for you. Paul writes that our "hope does not put us to shame." Because of God's unfailing love, our hope in him will be vindicated. Or, as the New Living Translation puts it, it "will not lead to disappointment." So why wouldn't you put your trust in God knowing that He loves you so much that He sent His son to die for you? And where else would you put your future hope than in God since you know He loves you and will protect you?

Now you know why God keeps pouring out His love on you. He wants you to put your faith and hope in His unfailing love every single day. Without the knowledge and experience of God's love, we could easily find ourselves hopeless.

The following story illustrates the importance of knowing God loves us:

A factory employee named Kenneth worked for the largest manufacturer in Illinois for twenty-four years. The wages and benefits paid at his factory were double what the average factory job paid in America. He had steady work. He was forty-four years old, yet he had never attended a union meeting. He was a contented, middle-class worker, until 1992.

From 1992 until 1994 you could find Kenneth at the end of the day shift marching through the factory, holding an American flag along with two other workers, chanting, "No contract. No peace. No contract. No peace." Kenneth called out the cadences for about one hundred middle-aged marchers.

What turned a contented worker into a thorn in this manufacturer's side? The turning point came in 1992 after the union had been on strike for nearly six months when the company threatened to replace its striking workers.

That did something to Kenneth. It turned him bitterly against his company. Kenneth angrily explains, "I finally realized two years ago, when they threatened to replace us, that as far as they are concerned, I am nothing to them."[2]

"I am nothing to them." Kenneth's whole attitude changed when he concluded, whether rightly or wrongly, that he had no worth to his boss or his company. He grew hopeless when he thought he was replaceable and that no one cared about him. Even the toughest laborer in America craves for someone to care. When he thought no one loved him, he lost his faith and grew hopeless.

There is only one place where we are assured that we are truly loved, and this is in a relationship with God. God values us and cares for us so much that even when we "went on strike" and rejected His will for our lives, instead of rejecting us in return, He sent His Son to die for our sins. No greater love will ever be shown than God sacrificing His only Son in our place. And God continually pours out His love into our hearts to fuel our hope and strengthen our faith.

Questions:

1. You read this line from R. Kent Hughes in today's devotion: "Our hearts have been filled to overflowing with divine affection." What thoughts does this statement bring to your mind concerning God's love for you?

2. How is your hope directly connected to the love God has poured into your heart?

3. In what specific ways can you put your hope in God knowing that, because He loves you, your hope will never be put to shame?

Day Fourteen

Hope

Our Lifeline

Hope is like a golden cord connecting you to Heaven.
The more you cling to this cord, the more God can bear the
weight of your burdens. Heaviness is not of God's Kingdom.
Cling to hope, and God's light will reach you through
the darkness.
Sarah Young[1]

Text: Psalm 62:5-7a (NLT)
[5] Let all that I am wait quietly before God, for my hope is in him. [6] He alone is my rock and my salvation, my fortress where I will not be shaken. [7] My victory and honor come from God alone.

Thoughts:
Psalm 62 was written by David in a season of trouble. David had seen enough warfare to know that God alone was his rock and salvation (Psalm 62:1). In Psalm 62, David refers to God as his salvation and refuge four times, and his rock three times. In verse 5, David says, ". . . my hope is in Him."

The word "hope" is *tiqvah*. The original meaning of *tiqvah* is "to stretch like a rope" and can be translated as "rope" or "cord." So the hope David refers to is his lifeline. His hope in God is the rope he holds to guide him through life's uncertainties. Beth Moore shares this application about *tiqvah*:

Every one of us is hanging on to something or someone for security. If it's someone or something other than God alone, you're hanging on by a thread – the wrong thread.[2]

It is hard to think about a cord of hope without thinking about Rahab in Joshua 2. And here is an interesting fact: The same word *tiqvah* is used two times in the story of Rahab. Here are the two Scriptures with *tiqvah* bolded:

Joshua 2:21 (ESV)
[21]And she said, "According to your words, so be it." Then she sent them away, and they departed. And she tied the scarlet **cord** in the window.

Joshua 2:18 (ESV)
[18] Behold, when we come into the land, you shall tie this scarlet **cord** in the window through which you let us down, and you shall gather into your house your father and mother, your brothers, and all your father's household.

Rahab used *tiqvah* to let down the Israelite spies from her house and allowed them to escape. The spies then instructed her to tie a scarlet cord (*tiqvah*) in the window as her hope for rescue. If she had the scarlet cord tied in her window, she and her entire family would be spared. Since hope and cord are used interchangeably for *tiqvah*, the spies tell Rahab to tie this scarlet hope in the window. When Israel attacked Jericho and the walls came tumbling down, Rahab and her family were saved. Their salvation was tied to the cord of hope. This is a picturesque description and illustration of our lifeline of hope.

The word *tiqvah* is used 34 times in the Old Testament, 13 of those times are found in the book of Job. Here are a few more times it is found in Scripture:

Psalm 71:5 (ESV)
⁵ For you, O Lord, are my **hope**, my trust, O Lord, from my youth.

Proverbs 23:18 (ESV)
¹⁸ Surely there is a future, and your **hope** will not be cut off.

Proverbs 24:14
¹⁴ Know that wisdom is such to your soul; if you find it, there will be a future, and your **hope** will not be cut off.

Jeremiah 29:11 (ESV)
¹¹ For I know the plans I have for you, declares the Lord, plans for welfare and not for evil, to give you a future and a **hope**.

Our hope connects us to God to give us comfort in our times of trouble. God is our salvation, refuge, and rock. He is our rope of hope. The Lord is our lifeline. Since we always have Him, we constantly have something solid to hold on to.

Questions:
1. What are your thoughts that *tiqvah* means both "hope" and "cord"?

2. Thinking on past experiences, what are some other lifelines besides God that you have tried to hold onto? What was the result?

3. In light of the cord of hope, how important is it that Scripture declares, "Your hope will not be cut off." (Proverbs 23:18, 24:14)?

Day Fifteen

Hope

When It Seems Like All Hope Is Lost

Hope means hoping when things are hopeless, or it is no virtue at all. As long as matters are really hopeful, hope is mere flattery or cliché. It is only when everything is hopeless that hope begins to have strength.

G.K. Chesterton[1]

Text: Matthew 12:15-21 (ESV)

[15] Jesus, aware of this, withdrew from there. And many followed him, and he healed them all [16] and ordered them not to make him known. [17] This was to fulfill what was spoken by the prophet Isaiah: [18] "Behold, my servant whom I have chosen, my beloved with whom my soul is well pleased. I will put my Spirit upon him, and he will proclaim justice to the Gentiles. [19] He will not quarrel or cry aloud, nor will anyone hear his voice in the streets; [20] a bruised reed he will not break, and a smoldering wick he will not quench, until he brings justice to victory; [21] and in his name the Gentiles will hope."

Thoughts:

Hope is one of the most important Christian virtues alongside faith and love. It is difficult to determine how many times the word *hope* is found in the Old Testament because no one word in the Hebrew Old Testament covers the Hebrew understanding of hope. According to the *New Wilson Old Testament*

Word Studies, six Hebrew words relate to the subject of hope. These words mean the following in our English translation: trust, refuge, patient waiting, confidence, expectation, and longing for.[2] These six words total 226 occurrences in the Old Testament.

Counting the number of times hope occurs in the New Testament is much easier because there is only one Greek word for it. The word is *elpis*, and it is found 53 times in the New Testament. Of those occurrences, Paul uses the word 37 times, with 13 of those coming from the Book of Romans. According to *Strong's Concordance*, *elpis* means expectation, trust, and confidence. It comes from the root word *elpo*, which means to anticipate with delight and to welcome. *Elpis* is an expectation of what is guaranteed.[3] It is used to describe anticipation of future events that are certain to come. Therefore, *hope* in the New Testament means looking forward with a reasonable expectation towards the future with confident assurance.

Elpis first appears in the New Testament in Matthew 12:21 when Matthew quotes from Isaiah 42:1-4 and says, *"and in His name, the Gentiles will hope."* Matthew 12 records Jesus healing a man with a shriveled hand on the Sabbath right in front of the Pharisees. Right after this occurred, the Pharisees began plotting how they might kill Jesus (Matthew 12:14). Aware of this, Jesus withdrew from that place. Many people still followed Jesus, and He healed the sick, warning people not to tell anybody who He was (Matthew 12:15-16). Then Matthew explained that this was to fulfill what had been spoken through the prophet Isaiah (Matthew 12:17).

Matthew quotes Isaiah 42:1-4 to get to the main focus on what was occurring in front of their eyes: Jesus was the fulfillment of prophecy and was their long-anticipated Messiah. This quotation from Isaiah showed that Jesus was indeed their King, but not the king everyone was expecting. Jews expected a king to come and reign and rule. Jesus would be a gentle ruler who would bring justice to the nations "without anyone hearing his voice in the streets" (Matthew 12:19).

Matthew 12:20 says, "A bruised reed He will not break, and a smoldering wick He will not quench, until He brings justice to victory." This bruised reed refers to the delicate lives of the ones Jesus would minister to. Jesus came to minister to people whose wick was about to go out. These people were hopeless and in despair, but their light would not go out before Jesus would bring them to victory. These terms describe a Savior who came to heal and save, not condemn and destroy. As Jesus had restored the shriveled man's hand, Jesus would restore the nations through His tender love and sacrificial death on the cross.

"And in His name the Gentiles will hope." The word for Gentiles in Greek is *ethne*. Our words ethnic and ethnicity come from this word. People from all nations, not just Jews, will one day put their hope in the name of Jesus.

Jews and Gentiles had waited for hundreds of years for a Messiah. They had waited through 400 silent years in the intertestamental period, the time between the events of the Old Testament and New. The people were being oppressed by the Roman government and their own legalistic religious leaders. Yet even in this long period of oppression and depression, the One in whom they hoped for was now here. Just when it seems like all hope is lost, Jesus appears as the hope for all nations!

Questions:

1. How significant is the first occurrence of the word hope in the New Testament? How important is it that the first time is a quote from the Old Testament?

2. How does a seemingly hopeless situation, actually strengthen your hope?

3. How does the following Scripture relate to the first use of hope in the New Testament found in Matthew 12:21?

Philippians 2:8-11 (ESV)
   [8] And being found in human form, he humbled himself by becoming obedient to the point of death, even death on a cross. [9] Therefore God has highly exalted him and bestowed on him the name that is above every name, [10] so that at the name of Jesus every knee should bow, in heaven and on earth and under the earth, [11] and every tongue confess that Jesus Christ is Lord, to the glory of God the Father.

Day Sixteen

Hope

Why We Never Give Up

*Hope sees a crown in reserve, mansions in readiness,
and Jesus himself preparing a place for us,
and by that rapturous sight hope sustains the soul
under the sorrows of the hour.*
Charles Spurgeon[1]

Text: 2 Corinthians 4:16-18 (NLT)

[16] That is why we never give up. Though our bodies are dying, our spirits are being renewed every day. [17] For our present troubles are small and won't last very long. Yet they produce for us a glory that vastly outweighs them and will last forever! [18] So we don't look at the troubles we can see now; rather, we fix our gaze on things that cannot be seen. For the things we see now will soon be gone, but the things we cannot see will last forever.

Thoughts:

The theme of 2 Corinthians 4 is proclaiming the light of Jesus Christ in a dark and broken world. Paul begins this chapter with these words: "Therefore, having this ministry by the mercy of God, we do not lose heart" (2 Corinthians 4:1). The word "therefore" refers to the confidence in God that Paul spoke of in 2 Corinthians 3 as he explained that we are ministers of a new covenant. As Paul speaks of our permanent glory, he reiterates that we are bold in serving Jesus because we have such hope (2 Corinthians 3:12). So we never give up or lose heart because of the certain confidence we have in what God has in store for us in Heaven. Observe the hope in Paul's words:

2 Corinthians 4:8-9 (ESV)

[8] We are afflicted in every way, but not crushed; perplexed, but not driven to despair; [9] persecuted, but not forsaken; struck down, but not destroyed;

Even surrounded by trouble, we have hope because of our future destination. That perspective leads Paul from speaking about burdened hearts (2 Corinthians 4:8-14) to a discussion of our blessed hope (2 Corinthians 4:16-18).

Paul starts his discussion on hope by saying, "That is why we never give up. Though our bodies are dying, our spirits are being renewed every day" (2 Corinthians 4:16). Paul contrasts what is happening to our physical bodies with what is occurring with our spirit. The word "dying" is a New Testament word that means to "corrupt" or "decay." Paul was physically aging, and the ministry was taking a toll on his body. Yet even while his body was beginning to wear out, his spirit was being renewed day by day. The word "renew" comes from a compound word consisting of two Greek words. One word means "completing a process" and the other word means "to move from one stage to a higher one." The second word can also mean "to make qualitatively new." Put together, Paul is saying that our spirit is being made new by moving daily from one stage to a higher one until the process is fully completed in us. Paul's hope was in his confidence that God was refining and perfecting his spirit the entire time his physical body was wearing out. What was most important to Paul was not his temporary physical body, but his eternal spirit.

Paul had learned to live one day at a time with a focus on the one aspect of his being that would last forever. Notice Paul's confidence in these words: "For our present troubles are small and won't last very long. Yet they produce for us a glory that vastly outweighs them and will last forever" (2 Corinthians 4:17). John Butler describes the great contrast in Paul's words:

> Note how Paul contrasted the dividends with the difficulties. The difficulties were *"small"* but the dividends were heavy (*"vastly outweighs"*). The difficulties were short (*"won't last long"*), the dividends long (*"forever"*). The difficulties were grievous (*"troubles"*), but the dividends were glorious (*"glory"*). This is a great perspective of trials.[2]

So, when Paul suffered affliction, he did not focus on the weight of his struggles, but on how heavy the future glory would be because he was going through these troubles.

Paul's incredible perspective of hope is revealed in his closing remarks. "So we don't look at the troubles we can see now; rather, we fix our gaze on things that cannot be seen. For the things we see now will soon be gone, but the things we cannot see will last forever" (2 Corinthians 4:18). We can see what is happening with our physical bodies. We witness with our own eyes the sufferings of this world. We cannot see with our physical eyes what God is doing to renew our spirit. Even though we can't see it with our eyes, we can put our hope and confidence that what we cannot see is eternal.

While we seek to take care of our physical bodies because they are the Temple of the Holy Spirit (1 Corinthians 6:19), eventually our bodies will wear out. So while we are slowly losing ground physically every day, our spirit is moving on to new heights, constantly being renewed until it finds its perfection in

Heaven with Jesus. That is why we never give up and we don't lose heart!

Questions:
1. How can your perspective (spiritual vision of what you can't see) give you hope in the midst of the suffering your physical eyes can see?

2. In what ways is the weight of the world's suffering considered light in comparison to the weight of our future glory?

3. How does Paul's life encourage you to never lose heart?

Day Seventeen

Hope

Sufferings Produce Hope

In Jesus Christ, God experienced the greatest depths of pain. Therefore, though Christianity does not provide the reason for each experience of pain, it provides deep resources for actually facing suffering with hope and courage rather than bitterness and despair.

Timothy Keller[1]

Text: Romans 5:1-5

[1] Therefore, since we have been justified by faith, we have peace with God through our Lord Jesus Christ. [2] Through him we have also obtained access by faith into this grace in which we stand, and we rejoice in hope of the glory of God. [3] Not only that, but we rejoice in our sufferings, knowing that suffering produces endurance, [4] and endurance produces character, and character produces hope, [5] and hope does not put us to shame, because God's love has been poured into our hearts through the Holy Spirit who has been given to us.

Thoughts:

Martin Luther said, "Romans is the chief part of the New Testament and is truly the purest gospel." John Piper declared that Romans is "the most important theological Christian work ever written." J. I. Packer wrote, "All roads in the Bible lead to Romans. When the message of Romans gets into a person's heart, there is no telling what may happen."[2]

One of the major themes of Romans is justification by faith (Romans 3-4). Justification by faith means that our right standing before God cannot result from the works that we have done. God requires a perfect righteousness that could never result from our performance of good works. The only righteousness acceptable to God is found in the work of His sinless Son, Jesus Christ. The righteousness that God requires for our justification is credited to our spiritual account when we place our faith in Jesus Christ.

Romans 5 begins by unveiling a further blessing that comes from justification by faith. When we are saved by faith, we obtain access to peace and grace. This leads us to celebrate with a hope-filled life knowing that we will see the glory of God. We would never be able to live with God's peace and have confident hope if our salvation could be obtained by our good works. We would always live in doubt and fear that our works aren't good enough. But since our salvation is dependent on what Jesus has done rather than our own efforts, we can live with complete confidence that Jesus' life, death, and resurrection satisfied the Father's requirement for the payment of our sins.

Romans 5:3-4 follows with an incredible truth that we can rejoice in our sufferings. Timothy Keller further clarifies this statement:

> Christians rejoice *in* suffering. There is no joy in the actual troubles themselves. God hates the pain and troubles of this life and so should we. Rather, a Christian knows that suffering will have beneficial results. A Christian is not a stoic, who faces suffering by just gritting their teeth. Christians "look through" the suffering to their certainties. They rest in the knowledge that troubles will only increase their enjoyment and appreciation of those certainties.[3]

To better understand this truth, you have to work through Paul's progression. Paul said that we can celebrate through our sufferings "knowing that suffering produces endurance, and endurance produces character, and character produces hope." So, you can discover from Paul's sequence that suffering ultimately produces hope.

Keller further explains how Romans 5:5 connects to Paul's overall discussion that we are saved by faith and not by works:

> Paul's addition of verse 5 right after verses 3 and 4 seems to mean that Christians who focus single-mindedly on prayer and obedience to God, and who therefore grow in confidence, will experience more of His love during suffering - an outpouring of God's love into our hearts. Many Christians testify that they feel more of God's presence and love during suffering because it makes them focus on and trust in Him more.
>
> Here is Paul's amazing assertion. When he shows that suffering starts a chain reaction that leads to hope, he is saying that the benefits of justification are not only not diminished by suffering, but they are also enlarged by it. In other words, if you face suffering with a clear grasp of justification by grace alone, your joy in that grace will deepen. On the other hand, if you face suffering with a mindset of justification by works, the suffering will break you, not make you.
>
> Consider how suffering affects people who are seeking salvation by works. Self-justifiers are always insecure at a deep level because they know they aren't living up to their standards, but they cannot admit it. So when suffering hits, they immediately feel they are being punished for their sins. They cannot take confidence in God's love (vs. 5). Since their belief that God loves them

is inadequately based, suffering shatters them. Suffer-ing drives them away from God, rather than toward Him. It is when we suffer that we discover what we are really trusting and hoping in, ourselves or God.[4]

A correct belief leads to a proper mindset. When we believe the truth that justification occurs through faith alone, we can understand more fully how suffering actually produces hope.

Questions:

1. Are you putting your trust in your good works or in what Jesus has already done? How does a works-based mentality leave you hopeless? How does a faith-based perspective pro-duce hope?

2. In what ways can you, as Timothy Keller said, "look through the sufferings to their certainties"?

3. How does the following statement give you hope in the midst of suffering?

> Hope for sufferers is rooted in the fact that they've not been singled out or forsaken but that what is painful has a purpose. If suffering has a purpose, then there is reason to believe that good things will come out of what doesn't seem good.[5]

Day Eighteen

Hope
_____

Hoping For What We Do Not See

Take comfort in knowing that God can see in the dark,
and the dark cannot overcome His light.
Sarah Frazer[1]

Text: Romans 8:18-25

[18] For I consider that the sufferings of this present time are not worth comparing with the glory that is to be revealed to us. [19] For the creation waits with eager longing for the revealing of the sons of God. [20] For the creation was subjected to futility, not willingly, but because of him who subjected it, in hope [21] that the creation itself will be set free from its bondage to corruption and obtain the freedom of the glory of the children of God. [22] For we know that the whole creation has been groaning together in the pains of childbirth until now. [23] And not only the creation, but we ourselves, who have the firstfruits of the Spirit, groan inwardly as we wait eagerly for adoption as sons, the redemption of our bodies. [24] For in this hope we were saved. Now hope that is seen is not hope. For who hopes for what he sees? [25] But if we hope for what we do not see, we wait for it with patience.

Thoughts:

Timothy George, in his book _Unseen Footprints_, tells the following story:

When I was a student at Harvard Divinity School, I learned preaching from Dr. Gardner Taylor, a pastor in New York City. I'll never forget those lectures. I remember him telling a story from when he was preaching in Louisiana during the Depression. Electricity was just coming into that part of the country, and he was out in a rural church that had just one little lightbulb hanging down from the ceiling to light up the whole sanctuary. He was preaching away, and in the middle of his sermon, the electricity went out. The building went pitch-black, and Dr. Taylor didn't know what to say, being a young preacher. He stumbled around until one of the elderly deacons sitting in the back of the church cried out, "Preach on, preacher! We can still see Jesus in the dark."[2]

When we find ourselves in the dark, we realize this could be the most hopeful time to see Jesus. The Good News of the Gospel is that whether or not we can see Him, He can always see us.

Romans 8 is one of the most beloved chapters in all of Scripture. The Apostle Paul begins and ends this chapter with multiple statements about the confidence and security we have in Christ. In Romans 8:18-25, Paul connects present suffering to future hope for both Christ's followers and creation itself. Because of our convictions of the power of Jesus' resurrection, we know that the believer and the world we live in are moving toward a brighter future.

Observe how Paul begins this section of Scripture: "For I consider that the sufferings of this present time are not worth comparing with the glory that is to be revealed to us." (Romans 8:18). John Piper explains this verse as follows:

That's what Paul wants us to believe with all our hearts. And you need to believe it in your heart and not just your head, because when the sufferings come it will take a deep, deep conviction and hope not to throw in the towel. You will be tempted to say: "If this is the payoff for trusting Christ, I'm done." If that were not a real temptation, Paul would not write this paragraph. He is writing to help us not throw away our hope in Christ when the miseries and groanings of this present time are overwhelming.[3]

Paul goes on to show that creatures (that's you and me) and creation (that's the world around us) have much in common. Both creatures and creation face the consequences of the Fall. Both creatures and creation are subject to disaster. Both creatures and creation experience darkness. Just as no one human is alone in struggling, all of creation is struggling, too, "subjected to futility" and "groaning together" (Romans 8:20, 22). But that's not the end of the story, for we have one final thing in common with creation: There is hope for redemption!

Though now creatures and creation are groaning, one day we will all be free. Verse 21 says, "creation itself will be set free from its bondage to corruption," and verse 23 says that we creatures will receive "adoption as sons, the redemption of our bodies." This is our certain hope, although we don't see it yet. And since we can't see it yet, we "wait for it with patience" (Romans 8:25).

As you face times of darkness, keep your hope in what you cannot see. One day we are going to have a new Heaven and a new Earth. One day soon, we are going to get a glorified body to worship a glorified Savior. Our final destination has no darkness, but it is constantly illuminated by the glory of God. Until then, you can be confident that we can still see Jesus in the dark. And you can be completely sure that He always sees you.

Questions:

1. What are your thoughts on the fact that you and God's creation are both currently experiencing groaning times in the dark?

2. In what ways can you live with greater hope in what you cannot see?

3. How can you develop stronger patience knowing the end goal God has for you?

Day Nineteen

Hope

God Is For Us

Regardless of where you are today, God is with you.
God is wooing you. God wants you to experience Him.
Whatever you are going through today,
you can find His joy and peace.
However distant your dreams may seem,
God is working things out, and today
is an important part of that process.
Lysa TerKeurst[1]

Text: Romans 8:31-32
[31] What then shall we say to these things? If God is for us, who can be against us? [32] He who did not spare his own Son but gave him up for us all, how will he not also with him graciously give us all things?

Thoughts:

What if you were yelling for help and no one could hear you? You could see them right there in front of you, but they could not hear your calls. Such was life for Rom Houben, a Belgian man in a coma. At least they thought he was in a coma. He said, "I was shouting, but no one could hear me."

In 2006 doctors used new scanning techniques and found that Rom, who had spent 23 years in this coma,

74

had normal brain function. Now he communicates with the world using a special keyboard.[2]

I can't think of a more hopeless feeling than being completely aware of your surroundings and totally unable to communicate with people around you. Unless, perhaps, it is the feeling of those who never realize that God is for them.

If you grew up watching Star Wars, you are very familiar with the phrase "May the force be with you." The problem is that trusting in a force only works in the movies. We don't need an imaginary force; we need somebody who walks with us and is for us. Every believer has that somebody in the person of Jesus Christ.

Romans 8:31 records two questions. The first question Paul poses is: "What then shall we say to these things?" The "these things" is the proof of God's unfailing and never-ending love found in the previous verses. This list includes the following: We have been adopted, called, justified, and glorified. Paul is declaring that God has good purposes for His children. In light of everything God has done for us, Paul asks the second question: "If God is for us, who can be against us?" The idea in context is, "If God loves you and has an ultimate purpose for your life, who can condemn you or try to defeat you? Who can take away what God has planned?" The obvious answer is, "No one." The Message Bible paraphrases Romans 8:31: "So, what do you think? With God on our side like this, how can we lose?" The New Century Version reads, "So what should we say about this? If God is with us, no one can defeat us."

Paul follows the two questions with a pinnacle statement about God's love for us followed by another question. He proclaims that God "did not spare His own Son but gave Him up for us all." God loved us so much that He sacrificed His own Son to allow all of us an opportunity to be saved. The statement sets up the question: "How will He not also with Him graciously give us all things?" Paul is arguing from the greater to the lesser. When we were lost, God gave us His Son in order to save us. This is the greatest gift that will ever be given, and God wouldn't start our spiritual life with the greatest gift and then not continue to give us what we need. Since we have been saved and adopted as His children, won't He continue to give us smaller gifts also? With that in mind, live daily with the certainty that since God is for you, you cannot lose.

Questions:
1. Consider this statement repeatedly in your mind and heart: "God is for me." When you contemplate that great truth, what is your response?

2. How does knowing that God gave His own Son give you hope for the future?

3. How does the following verse relate to today's Scripture?

Psalm 56:9 (ESV)
Then my enemies will turn back in the day when I call. This I know, because God is for me.

Day Twenty

Hope

More Than Conquerors

No matter what our circumstances, none of the sufferings of
this present time can separate us from the love of God.
This makes us conquerors and more.
David Guzik[1]

Text: Romans 8:35-39
[35] Who shall separate us from the love of Christ? Shall tribulation, or distress, or persecution, or famine, or nakedness, or
danger, or sword? [36] As it is written, "For your sake we are being
killed all the day long; we are regarded as sheep to be slaugh-
tered." [37] No, in all these things we are more than conquerors
through him who loved us. [38] For I am sure that neither death
nor life, nor angels nor rulers, nor things present nor things to
come, nor powers, [39] nor height nor depth, nor anything else in
all creation, will be able to separate us from the love of God in
Christ Jesus our Lord.

Thoughts:
   In the conclusion to Romans 8, Paul begins with a question:
"Who shall separate us from the love of Christ?" To a world full
of people – Christians included – who suffer from separation
anxiety, Paul's answer comes as the best news possible. Before
we get to the answer, let's look at Paul's list of scenarios that
might come against us and cause the separation we fear:

Tribulation, persecution, famine, nakedness, danger, and sword. Steven Runge writes:

> All of these are natural consequences of life in a yet-to-be-fully-redeemed world, but they have no bearing whatsoever on God's favor and love for us. No matter the circumstances, despite how we might feel, we must steadfastly rest in the truth that God is with us and for us. Nothing can separate us from His love.[2]

Did you catch the answer to Paul's question? He emphatically asserts that nothing can separate us from the love of Christ. He then takes his discussion to a greater height by adding, "In all these things we are more than conquerors through him who loved us." David Guzik beautifully describes this reality:

> How is the Christian more than a conqueror? He overcomes with a greater **power**, the power of Jesus. He overcomes with a greater **victory**, losing nothing even in the battle. He overcomes with a greater **love**, conquering enemies with love and converting persecutors with patience.[3]

However, there is even more to the "more than conquerors" statement. Paul said, "In all these things." It is through the sufferings and trials of life that God makes us "more than conquerors." Steven Runge's explanation is very beneficial to help us understand the magnitude of this terminology:

> Rather than the trials and opposition overcoming us or separating us from the love of Christ, the opposite is true. In Romans 8:37, Paul makes the audacious claim that we prevail - that we are more than conquerors.

How can this be? It is not because the trials and suffering disappear in the short term; they don't and won't. Rather, Paul's claim is based on the bigger picture outlined in Romans 8. All things work together for good - not by avoiding hardships - but by God guiding all things to accomplish His purposes. Since nothing can separate us from the love of God, and since no one can make an accusation stick against one of God's children, the short term doesn't matter. We may suffer, be imprisoned, and even be killed. But the God who was faithful enough to us to send His only Son will remain committed to finishing the job. Present battles indicate nothing about the overall war. God has already won - it is simply a matter of faithfully following Him as He does what He has promised - working all things together for good according to His larger plan. So when you feel tempted to be anxious about your status with God, instead remember the bigger picture.[4]

So nothing can separate us from the love of God. No difficulty has the power to defeat us. God takes the suffering in our lives to make us more than conquerors. What the evil one thinks will tear us down and make us less, God works for our good and His glory to make us more!

Questions:
1. How should those who know Christ face Paul's list of terrible situations found in Romans 8:35? Why is the believer's perspective vastly different from lost people who face the same struggles?

2. How are you living out the phrase "more than a conqueror"?

3. How does Paul's conclusion in verses 38-39 strengthen your hope in Jesus?

Romans 8:38-39 (ESV)

[38] For I am sure that neither death nor life, nor angels nor rulers, nor things present nor things to come, nor powers, [39] nor height nor depth, nor anything else in all creation, will be able to separate us from the love of God in Christ Jesus our Lord.

Day Twenty-One

Hope

Finding Renewed Strength

What comes into our minds when we think about God
is the most important thing about us.
A.W. Tozer[1]

Text: Isaiah 40:28-31 (NIV)
[28] Do you not know? Have you not heard? The Lord is the everlasting God, the Creator of the ends of the earth. He will not grow tired or weary, and his understanding no one can fathom. [29] He gives strength to the weary and increases the power of the weak. [30] Even youths grow tired and weary, and young men stumble and fall; [31] but those who hope in the Lord will renew their strength. They will soar on wings like eagles; they will run and not grow weary, they will walk and not be faint.

Thoughts:
The truths of Isaiah 40 can inspire us to find renewed strength. The prophet centers on the two incredible realities of God's size and strength. When you finally realize the size of God, you can fully rely on the strength of God.

In the first part of Isaiah 40, Isaiah shares several questions that reveal the greatness of God. These questions are asked while also implying, "Who can do these incredible feats but God?"

Isaiah 40:12 (NIV)

Who has measured the waters in the hollow of his hand, or with the breadth of his hand marked off the heavens? Who has held the dust of the earth in a basket, or weighed the mountains on the scales and the hills in a balance?

God measures the waters in the hollow of his hand. Earth's oceans contain 340 quintillion gallons of water (that number is 340 plus 18 zeros), yet Isaiah says God measures all the waters with the palm of His hand. That's how big our God is!

God has also marked off the heavens with the width of His hand. The known universe stretches more than 30 billion light years, which is 200 sextillion miles (that number is 200 plus 21 zeros). God's hand is a measuring stick comparable to an incomprehensible distance. That's how mighty our God is!

Isaiah 40:15 (NIV)

Surely the nations are like a drop in a bucket; they are regarded as dust on the scales; he weighs the islands as though they were fine dust.

The earth weighs 6 sextillion metric tons (that is 6 plus 21 zeros), yet to God that is just dust on the scales. That's how strong our God is!

Isaiah 40:26 (NIV)

Lift up your eyes and look to the heavens: Who created all these? He who brings out the starry host one by one and calls forth each of them by name. Because of his great power and mighty strength, not one of them is missing.

Scientists claim that there are at least 100 billion galaxies, and each galaxy is comprised of about 100 billion stars. To such mind-boggling math, Isaiah reminds us that God calls each star by name. That's how awesome our God is!

Just think about the Earth we live on and how God created it. The Earth spins at just over 1,000 miles per hour while it is orbiting the sun at 67,000 miles per hour. At the same time, the sun is traveling 43,500 miles per hour as it orbits around the center of the Milky Way Galaxy. God created the relationship between the Earth and the sun with precise detail to perfectly give us life on Earth. God is powerful and knows exactly what He is doing. What a mighty God we serve!

After Isaiah repeatedly reminds us how big God is, he closes chapter 40 with a challenge, starting in verse 28: "Do you not know? Have you not heard? The Lord is the everlasting God, the Creator of the ends of the earth. He will not grow tired or weary, and his understanding no one can fathom." God has the size and the strength, and He also never gets tired. He is the everlasting God. Not only is He creator God, but He rules over even the "ends of the earth." Nothing is outside His reach or beyond His control.

Our great God "gives strength to the weary and increases the power of the weak" (Isaiah 40:29). No matter how much we have to suffer, we can always place our hope in the Lord because we know He will renew our strength (Isaiah 40:31). The word for "renew" in the Hebrew actually means "to exchange." Those who trust in the Lord have the privilege of exchanging their weakness for God's strength.

Notice the descending order of the life of faith. "They will soar on wings like eagles; they will run and not grow weary, they will walk and not be faint" (Isaiah 40:31b).

The order goes from soaring to running and ends with walking. We think of life in the reverse order. We believe that if we walk with the Lord long enough, we will start to run with Him and eventually soar with Him. However, the order in Isaiah

40:31 is an accurate description of the Christian life. The man or woman of faith may sometimes soar on eagle's wings or run without growing weary, but most of the time he merely walks by faith. The real test of faith comes not when he flies or runs, but when he must slowly push forward. It is in the monotony and routine of everyday life that greater hope in the Lord is required. As we consider the greatness of God, we can trust Him to daily renew our strength.

Questions:

1. How does knowing who God is give us more hope to rely on Him?

2. What are your thoughts on exchanging your weakness for His strength?

3. What does it mean to you that Isaiah has the order of hope from soaring to running to walking?

Day Twenty-Two

Hope

Hope Has a Name - Jesus

"And His name will be the hope of all the world."
Matthew 12:21 (NLT)

Text: Galatians 4:4-5
⁴ But when the fullness of time had come, God sent forth his Son, born of woman, born under the law, ⁵ to redeem those who were under the law, so that we might receive adoption as sons.

Thoughts:
Today begins the fourth week of our series on biblical hope. This week we turn our attention to the hope found when God sent His Son Jesus into the world. The following story illustrates the hope that only Christ can bring:

Port Authority Police Officers Will Jimeno and John McLoughlin were the last two people rescued from the World Trade Center after the September 11 terrorist attack. For Will Jimeno, that tragic day represents a defining moment in his Christian faith.

Jimeno, McLoughlin, and three other officers entered Tower 1 to rescue civilians. But when they got inside, the building collapsed. McLoughlin and Jimeno were pinned under large blocks of concrete rubble and twisted steel. The other three officers were killed.

For the next ten hours, Jimeno and his partner fought pain and thirst inside a concrete tomb swirling with dust and smoke. At times, ruptured gas lines would hurl fireballs into the ruins, threatening to burn the two men to death. In another terrifying moment, heat from the fireballs "cooked off" the ammunition inside the firearm of a fallen officer, sending fifteen bullets ricocheting around the chamber.

Jimeno's hope began to falter. "I was exhausted. I had done everything as a police officer that I could do, and everything as a human being," he said. "I just knew I was going to die." Just then, Jimeno saw a figure coming toward him through the rubble. "He wore a glowing white robe and a rope belt," Jimeno said. "I couldn't see his face, but I knew it was Jesus."

The vision filled Jimeno with hope. "I had this resurgence of the will to fight," he said. Turning toward McLoughlin, he yelled, "We're going to get out of here." Several hours later, U.S. Marines and NYPD rescue workers lifted the men out of their concrete prison.[1]

In Jimeno's horrible situation, hope came at just the right time. In addition, his hope had a name – Jesus.

Likewise, Scripture declares, "When the right time came, God sent His Son" (Galatians 4:4 NLT). Timing is everything. Hitters in baseball know how crucial timing is. A quarterback throwing to a speedy receiver understands the importance of timing. Musicians and singers will also tell you that timing is everything. God's timing is perfect, and He prepared the exact time in history to send Jesus into the world.

Paul writes, "When the fullness of time had come, God sent forth His Son." The phrase "fullness of time" is a Greek expression that speaks of something complete and fully developed like a ripe apple that is ready to be picked or a pregnant woman who is ready to deliver her baby. This expression refers to an appointed time. Why wasn't Jesus born during the days of Abraham, Isaac, or Jacob? Why didn't God send His Son during the time of Moses, Joshua, or David? The answer is that it wasn't the right time.

God sent His Son into the world when the world's stage was perfectly set. Jesus wasn't born an hour late or a minute too early. Christ came at the perfect time. For thousands of years, the Jews had waited for a Messiah. The Gentiles had long awaited a Savior. But a little over 2,000 years ago, on the exact date and in the appointed place, God said, "The perfect time is now, and the wait is over."

God's timing was perfect on several levels. First, the timing was right culturally. Jesus was sent into the world when the Roman Empire was in charge. Greek had just been adopted as the universal language. This would be the first time in history that there was one common language that everybody could speak and understand. So when the Gospels and the letters of Paul, Peter, and James were all written in Greek, everyone in the known world at that time could understand the Good News of Jesus.

The timing was also politically perfect. Because the Roman Empire was so strong, they were able to establish an unprecedented time of peace. A period of over 200 years, from 27 BC until 180 AD, was known as Pax Romana, which means, "Roman peace." Jesus was born at a time when peace reigned universally across the Roman Empire. Because no wars were being fought, the Romans had the time and resources to build an infrastructure of roads that had never been seen before. This led to the famous phrase, "All roads lead to Rome." During these 200 years, the church could go anywhere and preach the Gospel to a world that was at peace.

The timing was also spiritually perfect. Notice how Paul emphasizes "the law" twice in Galatians 4:4-5: "Born of woman, born under the law, to redeem those who were under the law, so that we might receive adoption as sons." In the past, God's people had continually broken His law. Because of this disobedience, they were divided and dispersed throughout the region. The consequences of their sin humbled them and caused them to long for God again. Therefore, during the time of Jesus' birth, Jews returned to their monotheistic roots and began teaching the law of the Old Testament again. Because Rome was in charge, they could no longer have a temple, so they built synagogues. If you know the history of where Christianity began, you know that every time Paul went to a foreign city, he always went to a synagogue. Paul knew that there he would find a congregation full of Jews studying the Old Testament who were looking for the promised Messiah.

At the perfect right time, God sent forth the hope that He had promised. After the Jews had waited and it appeared that all hope was lost, God sent them the greatest hope this world has ever known. This hope has a name, and that name is Jesus, the long-awaited Messiah.

Questions:

1. How important is the right timing? What are your thoughts on God's perfect timing?

2. How does Ecclesiastes 3:1-2a relate to today's devotion?

[1]For everything there is a season, and a time for
every matter under heaven: [2]a time to be born, . . .

3. How does this anonymous quote encourage you to put your
hope in Jesus?

"God has perfect timing; never early, never late.
It takes a little patience, and it takes a lot of faith,
but it's worth the wait."

Day Twenty-Three

Hope

Tabernacled Among Us

Christianity does not begin with our pursuit of Christ.
It begins with Christ's pursuit of us.
Anonymous

The Word of the Father by whom all time was created
was made flesh and born in time for us. The maker of man
became man that He the bread might be hungry, that He the
fountain might thirst, that He the way might be wearied in the
journey, that He the truth might be accused by false witnesses,
that He the just might be condemned by the unjust, that He
the foundation might be suspended on a cross,
and that He the life, might die.
Augustine[1]

Text: John 1:14
[14] And the Word became flesh and dwelt among us, and we
have seen his glory, glory as of the only Son from the Father, full
of grace and truth.

Thoughts:
"The Word became flesh and dwelt among us." The term
dwelt means "to live in a tent." In other words, Jesus tab-
ernacled among us. Everything God's presence was in the
Old Testament Tabernacle, Christ is now to us through His

incarnation. Jesus came to earth to save and redeem mankind. He left Heaven so that we could experience His presence in our hearts.

John's wording here is specific for a significant reason: "We have seen His glory, glory as of the only Son from the Father." The *shekinah* glory that filled the Tabernacle comes to mind. The presence of God would fill the Old Testament Tabernacle so gloriously that Moses was not even able to enter it. It was so full of God that there was no room for anybody else.

Only the high priest had the privilege of going into the holy of holies one time a year and experiencing a closeness with God. Jesus was born into the world so that by His death God could grant everyone access to God's glorious presence. The same presence that was in the Tabernacle is experienced with Jesus as His Spirit lives in us. When Jesus left His home in Heaven, He made room for all of us to encounter the glory of God.

Never forget that the "Word (Jesus) became flesh." In Colossians 2:9 (NLT), Paul adds clarification to John's emphasis: "For in Christ lives all the fullness of God in a human body." The fullness of God dwells in the person of Jesus Christ. As someone once said, "Jesus is God with skin on." God robed His Son in flesh so Jesus could walk among us.

Notice the emphasis on Jesus' flesh in the following Scriptures:

Hebrews 2:14-15 (NLT)
¹⁴ Because God's children are human beings - made of flesh and blood - the Son also became flesh and blood. For only as a human being could he die, and only by dying could he break the power of the devil, who had the power of death. ¹⁵ Only in this way could he set free all who have lived their lives as slaves to the fear of dying.

Philippians 2:6-8 (ESV)

⁶ [Christ Jesus} though he was in the form of God, did not count equality with God a thing to be grasped, ⁷ but emptied himself, by taking the form of a servant, being born in the likeness of men. ⁸ And being found in human form, he humbled himself by becoming obedient to the point of death, even death on a cross.

Hebrews 4:15 (ESV)

¹⁵ For we do not have a high priest who is unable to sympathize with our weaknesses, but one who in every respect has been tempted as we are, yet without sin.

Jesus came in flesh and blood and lived a perfect sinless life to die for our sinful flesh. Because He took on flesh, He knows our struggles. Because Jesus was clothed with humanity, He knows our pain. Christ was tempted in every way we are, yet He did not sin. This means we have a Savior who can identify with those He came to rescue.

The incarnation is the invitation for celebration. Since there was no way for humanity to get to God, God sent Jesus to us. Jesus left Heaven and came down to Earth so that we could leave Earth one day and go to Heaven. Jesus came to dwell among us, and He came to die. Because no animal sacrifice could cover our sin, Jesus became the sacrifice as the Passover Lamb. Jesus lived a sinless life and died a sacrificial death so that we could be forgiven of all our sins and have everlasting life.

I have often wondered why there was no room in Bethlehem for Jesus when He came in the flesh. You would think that the God of the universe would have reserved a room for His only Son. At least somebody should have made room for Him. May His birth remind you to make room for Jesus.

Questions:

1. Is your life too full of the things of this world that there is no room for Jesus?

2. How can you make room today for His glory to fill your life?

3. How does the fact that Jesus was fully human and fully God help you live with greater hope today?

Day Twenty-Four

Hope

Signs of Our Savior

Why do some people 'find' God in a way that others do not?
Why does God manifest His Presence to some and let multi-
tudes of others struggle along in the half-light of imperfect
Christian experience? Of course, the will of God is the same for
all. He has no favorites within His household. All He has ever
done for any of His children He will do for all of His children.
The difference lies not with God but with us.
A.W. Tozer[1]

Text: Isaiah 7:14
[14] Therefore the Lord Himself will give you a sign. Behold, the virgin shall conceive and bear a son, and shall call his name Immanuel.

Thoughts:
Sometimes when you are surrounded by the familiar, you
can miss the obvious. Isaiah 7:14 is a Scripture often quoted
around Christmas. It is a great verse on the virgin birth of Jesus
and reminds us that His name is Immanuel, which means "God
is with us."

If you grew up around church, you already know everything
you just read. But have you ever studied the context of this
verse? And what is the sign referred to in this verse? Great questions, right?

First, look at the details surrounding Isaiah's statement about the virgin birth. At the time Isaiah was writing, Judah was ruled by an evil king named Ahaz. King Ahaz became king at age 20 and ruled for 20 years from 735 – 715 BC. During Isaiah 7-10, Ahaz is in a terrible situation. Ephraim and Syria were attacking Jerusalem and seeking to overthrow King Ahaz. God sends Isaiah to King Ahaz to declare to him that his attackers will fail and be destroyed. Then God tells Ahaz to ask for a sign, but Ahaz refuses. So God gives him one anyway. That's where Isaiah 7:14 comes in: "Therefore the Lord Himself will give you a sign. Behold, the virgin shall conceive and bear a son, and shall call his name Immanuel."

Wait just one minute. How is Isaiah's prophecy about Jesus being born of a virgin a sign for Ahaz? Remember, it was 700 BC, so Jesus would not be born for another 700 years!

The word translated as "virgin" in Isaiah 7:14 is *almah*. This Hebrew word can mean "virgin," but it also can describe a "young woman of marrying age," depending on context.

Therefore, the child to be born was both an immediate sign in Ahaz's time and a future prophecy that foreshadowed the virgin birth of Jesus Christ.

Notice the immediate fulfillment of a child being born in Ahaz's time by looking at Isaiah 7:15-16 (NIV):

> [15] He will be eating curds and honey when he knows enough to reject the wrong and choose the right, [16] for before the boy knows enough to reject the wrong and choose the right, the land of the two kings you dread will be laid waste.

The birth of this child is a sign from God guaranteeing that Judah would not be destroyed by Syria and Ephraim. If your city was being attacked by Ephraim and Syria, wouldn't you

95

want the message to be "God help us"? Yet the most important thing you need to know is that God is with you!

However, the major point of this prophecy is that it prefigured the birth of the virgin-born Son of God, Jesus Christ. Matthew would later realize the foreshadowing of Jesus found in Isaiah 7:14. Observe Matthew 1:23, "Behold, the virgin shall conceive and bear a son, and they shall call his name Immanuel." As in Ahaz's day, the most important message for the whole world is "God is with us." The sign is the message found in God's name.

Therefore, Isaiah 7:14 has two messages found in the sign of one name. One message was for the present time, signaling the defeat of two evil nations. The other was for all time, signaling the defeat of sin, death, and the devil. The sign stayed the same. No matter how big our problems are in the present and the future, God is with us!

I am so glad that God showed me the two-fold meaning of His prophecy in Isaiah 7:14. For so long I had missed the obvious because of the familiar. The most important lesson for today is not to miss the sign of your Savior because you have grown too comfortable with the familiar. The same God who can give a prophecy that can be fulfilled 700 years apart can fill your heart with hope. Praise Jesus today and every day remembering that His name is Immanuel – God is with us!

Questions:
1. In what ways have you missed some of the signs that Jesus is your Savior?

2. How does a deeper study of Isaiah 7:14 give you more hope in the power of God?

3. How would you answer Tozer's question that began today's devotion?

Why do some people 'find' God in a way that others do not?

Day Twenty-Five

Hope

The Miracle Birth of Jesus

The birth of Jesus is the sunrise in the Bible.
Henry Van Dyke[1]

Text: Luke 1:30-33

[30] And the angel said to her, "Do not be afraid, Mary, for you have found favor with God. [31] And behold, you will conceive in your womb and bear a son, and you shall call his name Jesus. [32] He will be great and will be called the Son of the Most High. And the Lord God will give to him the throne of his father David, [33] and he will reign over the house of Jacob forever, and of his kingdom there will be no end."

Thoughts:

The doctor said, "If you are a believer in miracles, this would be one." The doctor was talking about Alcides Moreno. By every law of physics and medicine, Moreno should have died. Moreno was a window washer in Manhattan. He rode platforms with his brother Edgar high into the sky to wash skyscrapers. From there he could look down to see the pavement far below where the people looked like ants. On December 7, 2007, catastrophe struck the Moreno family. As the brothers worked on the forty-seventh story of a high-rise, their platform collapsed, and Alcides and Edgar fell from the sky.

If you are a believer in miracles, this would be one. No, Alcides Moreno didn't land on a passing airplane or catch his shirt on a flagpole or have anything else amazing happen like you see in the movies; he fell the entire forty-seven stories to the pavement below. As would be expected, his brother Edgar died from the fall, but somehow Alcides did not. He lived. For two weeks he hung on to life by a thread. Then, on Christmas Day, he spoke and reached out to touch his nurse's face. One month later, the doctors were saying that he would probably walk again someday.

If you are a believer in miracles, this would be one. In the beginning of the human race, Adam also fell from a great height. From sinless glory in the image of God, Adam rebelled against God and fell into sin, death, and judgment, and in this terrible fall, he brought with him the whole human race.[2]

But "God so loved the world that he gave His one and only Son, that whoever believes in Him shall not perish but have eternal life" (John 3:16). God the Son left the heights of Heaven and descended to the earth to become a man. He lived a sinless life and then willingly went to the cross to die for the sins of Adam's fallen race. On the third day, He rose from the dead to make it possible for every fallen person to rise again one day and live forever. If you are a believer in miracles, this would be the one.

The miracle of salvation began with the virgin birth of our Savior Jesus Christ. Mary found favor with God and got more than just a front-row seat for the miracle of the incarnation. For nine months, she carried baby Jesus inside of her. The mother of Jesus, who would later kneel at His feet at the cross, felt His feet kick inside of her womb.

When the angel announced that Mary would bear a Son, he told her, "He will be great and will be called the Son of the Most High." Mary is carrying a Son who has a Father called "The Most High God." Jesus, who has no beginning and no end, already existed as eternal God. So, while God provided His divinity, the virgin birth through Mary will lead to His humanity. The virgin-born Son of God will live a sinless life and will be able to pay the ultimate sacrifice for our sins.

After Jesus' virgin birth, sinless life, sacrificial death, and powerful resurrection, He will reign victorious for all eternity. Every believer who endures will one day reign with Him (2 Timothy 2:12). Our hope for eternity hinges on the miraculous virgin birth of Jesus. If you are a believer in miracles, this would be the one!

Questions:
1. How does the miracle of the virgin set up all the other miracles of Jesus?

2. Imagine what Mary felt as she carried baby Jesus inside of her during the months before His birth. How do these thoughts encourage you as a believer knowing that Christ forever lives in you?

3. What are your thoughts on the following statement?

The Son of God became man to enable men to become the sons of God. – C.S. Lewis[3]

Day Twenty-Six

Hope

Contagious Hope

Hope is contagious.
When you have enough of it, it spreads naturally.
Anonymous

Text: Luke 2:8-20

⁸ And in the same region there were shepherds out in the field, keeping watch over their flock by night. ⁹ And an angel of the Lord appeared to them, and the glory of the Lord shone around them, and they were filled with great fear. ¹⁰ And the angel said to them, "Fear not, for behold, I bring you good news of great joy that will be for all the people. ¹¹ For unto you is born this day in the city of David a Savior, who is Christ the Lord. ¹² And this will be a sign for you: you will find a baby wrapped in swaddling cloths and lying in a manger." ¹³ And suddenly there was with the angel a multitude of the heavenly host praising God and saying, ¹⁴ "Glory to God in the highest, and on earth peace among those with whom he is pleased!" ¹⁵ When the angels went away from them into heaven, the shepherds said to one another, "Let us go over to Bethlehem and see this thing that has happened, which the Lord has made known to us." ¹⁶ And they went with haste and found Mary and Joseph, and the baby lying in a manger. ¹⁷ And when they saw it, they made known the saying that had been told them concerning this child. ¹⁸ And all who heard it wondered at what

the shepherds told them. [19] But Mary treasured up all these things, pondering them in her heart. [20] And the shepherds returned, glorifying and praising God for all they had heard and seen, as it had been told them.

Thoughts:

The announcement of Jesus' birth was both powerfully supernatural and extremely relational. The authors of the *Life Application Bible Commentary* provide great insight from Luke's account of the announcement of Jesus' birth:

> The angel Gabriel had announced the coming births of John and Jesus. Here a host of angels announced the "good news" of Jesus' birth and broke out into exuberant praise. The angels called the baby Jesus the promised Messiah - the Savior. Such an announcement was a typical proclamation of the birth of a child to the royal family - for Augustus himself had been called a "savior" at his birth. But while the announcement of Augustus's birth would have been first delivered to the members of the Roman Senate and other dignitaries, the privilege of hearing about Jesus' birth first was given to ordinary shepherds.[1]

Luke 2 is filled with the glory of the Lord and the joy of His people. This Scripture is overflowing with anticipation and worship. In verse 12, there is a host of angels praising God. In verse 19, Mary is pondering everything that is happening in her heart. In verse 20, the shepherds return glorifying and praising God. Excitement filled the air around Jesus' birth!

When was the last time you got really excited about something? In your enthusiasm, did you rush off to tell somebody about it? When someone tells us good news that fills our hearts with joy, it is difficult to keep it to ourselves. We have to share what excites us.

In Luke 2, we see this to be true for the shepherds who hurried to Bethlehem to meet Jesus. In biblical times, shepherds found themselves on the lowest rung of their society's ladder. Because they spent every day with animals, their vocation was considered unclean. One of the many things I love about God is who He chooses to do life with. God chose to share the miracle of His Son's birth with the outcasts of society. The lowly shepherds were the first group of people to see the long-awaited Messiah.

What's even more remarkable was the shepherds' response. They had to immediately share the good news they had just heard. There was no way they could keep their joy to themselves. They had to talk about the amazing hope of Jesus that was now available to the entire world.

One thing I know is that despair and hope are both contagious. If you get around a bunch of negative people, it doesn't take long for you to feel depressed. However, if you get around people who are excited about Jesus, it fires you up about the goodness of God.

Never forget that hope is contagious. Based on the promises and faithfulness of God, every believer should be filled with expectation that something incredible is coming in their future. If our hope is founded in Jesus, that hope cannot be stopped or contained.

The Life Application Bible Commentary offers some final wisdom for applying Luke 2 to our daily lives:

> The angels gave the shepherds a sign. They would find their Savior in "a manger" - a sign of not only Jesus' identity but also His humble circumstances. By highlighting the modest character of Jesus' birth, Luke set

the stage for the bulk of his narrative: a story describing how Jesus gathered twelve common Israelite men to help Him minister to the ordinary people of Israel. The shepherds' response to the angels' announcement is similar to Mary's: they "hurried off" to see what God was accomplishing and returned, praising Him (Luke 1:39, 46–56; 2:16, 20). God still breaks into ordinary lives, even yours. Follow His instructions, praising Him for using you to accomplish His will.[2]

God sent His Son to Earth so that He could provide us forgiveness of our sins and conquer death forever. Jesus' life, death, and resurrection made it possible for fallen people to be restored back into a right relationship with God. Everything Jesus did and continues to do gives us hope. The Gospel is the greatest news ever and we cannot keep it to ourselves. As you continue to follow Jesus, remember that His hope is contagious. May that hope cause us to celebrate Christ every day of our lives.

Questions:
1. God revealed the long-awaited Savior first to shepherds. How does that truth encourage you? What does that reveal about God?

2. In what ways are you celebrating the Good News of Jesus Christ?

3. Can other people see the hope of Jesus in your life?

Day Twenty-Seven

Hope

The Giver of Hope

Optimism is a wish without warrant;
Christian Hope is a certainty, guaranteed by God Himself.
Optimism reflects ignorance as to whether good things will
ever actually come. Christian hope expresses knowledge that
every day of his life, and every moment beyond it,
the believer can say with truth, on the basis of God's
own commitment, that the best is yet to come.
J. I. Packer[1]

Text: John 3:16
[16] "For God so loved the world, that he gave his only Son, that whoever believes in him should not perish but have eternal life."

Thoughts:
John 3:16 is by far the most well-known verse in all of Scripture. It has been called "the golden text of the Bible." Concerning John 3:16, John Phillips writes:

We have now arrived at the great metropolis of gospel truth. No other single statement in the Bible so aptly sums up God's redemptive purpose in Christ for the human race. Volumes have been written on it. Its each and every word has been weighed and examined and marveled at and preached on. Who will ever know until the judgment seat of Christ how many millions of Adam's ruined race have found their way to heaven by the discovery of John 3:16?[2]

One of the many facets of truth found in this one verse is the giving love of God. How much does God love you? He loves you so much that He gave the greatest gift He could ever give. He "gave His only Son." The reason God gave His only Son was He "so" loved the world. The greatest gift ever given was given out of the greatest love ever known. God loved us so much that He gave us the gift of salvation.

Willard Swartley describes God's gift of love and Jesus' gift of Himself:

> This giving is radical, unreserved, risky, and painful. It's the story we know so well, but we often fail to be moved by its sublime and simple truth: God loves so much that He gave what He cherished most, His only Son. Paul's great hymn in Philippians 2:5–11 complements this truth by telling the story from the Son's side. The Son willingly gives Himself, even unto death, unto death on a cross for our salvation. Salvation is a gift. Further, it is for *all*: the term *whoever* denotes a potential response for anyone to receive this gift.[3]

Jesus says John 3:16 to Nicodemus, a leading religious ruler. We know from John 3:2 that Nicodemus came to Jesus at night. So, the greatest statement of hope found in all of Scripture was first given in the dark of night. Because God sent His Son Jesus, and because Jesus died on the cross and rose again, we always have hope no matter how dark this world gets. Therefore, we place our hope in God who is the greatest giver. He is the greatest giver because He gives the greatest gifts. His greatest gift involved the sacrificial death of His only Son. That greatest gift provides our salvation.

The Bible refers to salvation as a gift. Paul wrote these words to believers in Rome:

Romans 6:23 (ESV)

²³ For the wages of sin is death, but the free gift of God is eternal life in Christ Jesus our Lord.

John 3:16 along with Romans 6:23 reveals two important truths about God's gift of salvation. First, salvation is a costly gift. Think about it this way. If you wanted to show your love to someone by buying them a great gift, you would first have to purchase the gift. The nicer the gift, the more it would cost you. This gift would be free to the recipient, but it costs you to give it. This is also true with God's gift of salvation. It is a free gift for us, but it cost God the life of His only Son. Salvation is the most valuable gift ever given and it came at an extremely high cost. God paid for our salvation with the death of His Son.

There is a second truth about God's gift of salvation. Since it is a gift, it must be received. Like any other gift, it doesn't become yours until you accept it. You could refuse to accept a gift someone was attempting to give you. It would be rude, but a gift can be refused.

Why would anyone refuse to accept God's gift of salvation? It costs everything for God to give it, and it is free for you to receive it. If you haven't accepted this incredible gift, reach out by faith and receive God's gift of salvation today.

The greatest verse in Scripture also provides our greatest assurance. When we trust in Jesus and receive His gift of salvation, we can know with certainty that we will "not perish but have eternal life." Since God gave the gift of salvation, God is the ultimate giver of hope.

Questions:

1. Besides salvation, what is the greatest gift you have ever received? Why is the gift great and what did it cost someone to give it to you?

2. Why is salvation being a gift crucial to our understanding of the doctrine of salvation?

3. How is your greatest hope tied to God's greatest gift?

Day Twenty-Eight

Hope

Christ in You, the Hope of Glory

Paul's great definition of a Christian was "a person **in** Christ."
He used that picture over and over again in his writings.
What a revelation: Christ in you, the hope of glory!
Maxie Dunnam and Lloyd Ogilvie[1]

Text: Colossians 1:26-27
[26] the mystery hidden for ages and generations but now revealed to his saints. [27] To them God chose to make known how great among the Gentiles are the riches of the glory of this mystery, which is Christ in you, the hope of glory.

Thoughts:
Paul described our eternal destiny with Christ with the phrase "the hope of glory." "The hope of glory" is the ultimate fulfillment of God's promise to restore every believer and His creation. This hope is not a wishful belief, but the sure expectation of knowing that God is transforming us into His image as He is preparing us for Heaven.

Paul clarifies that your "hope of glory" is "Christ in you." Our only hope for glory comes from Christ living in us. "Christ in you" expresses the central identity of every follower of God. It declares that believers partake in a personal relationship with Jesus Christ who dwells within them through the power of the Holy Spirit.

Steven Cole explains a detail of Paul's message that is often overlooked and then provides great application to our hope for glory:

> When Paul says, "Christ in you" (Colossians 1:27), he means, in this context, "Christ in you Gentiles." For Paul, this was a glorious truth, but I fear that we don't appreciate it as much as we should. Before the cross of Christ, which opened the gospel to both Jews and Gentiles on equal standing, Gentiles were at best second-class citizens in the kingdom. Gentiles could become proselytes to Judaism, but they could only enter into the court of the women and Gentiles in the Temple. They could not go into the inner court where the Jewish men went. There was a waist-high wall of partition that separated them. Before his conversion, Paul was at the forefront of perpetuating this discrimination.
>
> But once Paul was saved, God revealed to him that the Gentiles were fellow heirs of the gospel with the Jews. The wall of partition is removed in Christ (Ephesians 2:14). As he writes in Colossians 3:11, "There is no distinction between Greek and Jew, circumcised and uncircumcised, barbarian, Scythian, slave and freeman, but Christ is all, and in all." Christ is in every believer and every believer is in Christ!
>
> Paul says that the riches of the glory of the gospel is, "Christ in you, the hope of glory." I know that you all know that if you have believed in Jesus Christ, He dwells in you and you're going to heaven. I know it, too. But do we really know it?
>
> If we really knew that the living Christ was in us this past week and that we will one day be with Him in glory, would things have gone any differently? Would we have

been impatient, frustrated, angry, or depressed if we had stopped to consider that Christ is living in us, and we're destined to share His glory? Would we have spent our time as we spent it if we had been aware of His holy presence in our hearts and thought about being with Him in glory? Would we have grown cold in our devotion to Him and lacked the motivation to read His Word and to pray if we had felt the reality of Christ dwelling in our hearts and had our hope set on the glory ahead? Christianity is not primarily rules or religious ideas; it's a personal relationship with the living, indwelling Christ, who has called us to share His glory. We exalt Him when we experience and proclaim that message.[2]

Let's live daily with the incredible assurance that comes from having Christ in us, our "hope of glory."

Questions:
1. How does "Christ in you" fill you with hope when the world around you seems hopeless?

2. Taking Steven Cole's challenge to heart, what are some practical steps you can take this week to live out the reality that Christ is in you?

3. How does the following N.T. Wright quote relate to today's devotion?

> God's secret plan is not, for Paul, a timetable of events, but a person.[3]

Day Twenty-Nine

Hope

Rejoice in Hope

There is one thing that
gives radiance to everything.
It is the idea of something around the corner.
G.K. Chesterton[1]

Text: Romans 12:12
[12] Rejoice in hope, be patient in tribulation, be constant in prayer.

Thoughts:
In the first eleven chapters of Romans, Paul discusses the doctrines of the Christian faith. Then, Romans 12 transitions into the application of those doctrines. Chapter 12 begins with these words:

Romans 12:1-2 (NIV)
[1] Therefore, I urge you, brothers and sisters, in view of God's mercy, to offer your bodies as a living sacrifice, holy and pleasing to God - this is your true and proper worship. [2] Do not conform to the pattern of this world, but be transformed by the renewing of your mind. Then you will be able to test and approve what God's will is - His good, pleasing and perfect will.

What we believe changes the way we behave. Therefore, Paul begins to discuss behavior that should characterize every believer in Christ. He begins by explaining that Christians should humbly serve as part of the Body of Christ (Romans 12:3-8). Next, Paul describes what love in action looks like for every Christ-follower (Romans 8:9-21). It is in this section, that we find the Scripture for today's devotion.

Romans 12:12 contains three actions that describe how Christian love is displayed. Rather than being commands, these three succinct statements are all present active participles. They can be translated as: "rejoicing in hope, being patient in tribulation, and being constant in prayer." By describing them as participles, Paul is inferring that every believer has a daily choice to live with these powerful principles in their everyday lives.

In his book *Forged by Fire*, Bob Reccord shares a story out of his own difficult circumstances. His testimony clearly illustrates Paul's threefold message: "Rejoice in hope, be patient in tribulation, and be constant in prayer."

> I had a severe cervical spinal injury. The pain was so excruciating that the hospital staff couldn't do an MRI until I was significantly sedated. The MRI showed significant damage at three major points in the cervical area. Because of the swelling of injured nerve bundles, the only way I could relieve the pain was to use a strong, prescribed narcotic and to lie on bags of ice. Sleep, what little there was, came only by sitting in a reclining chair.
>
> Approximately forty-eight hours from the onset of the injury, doctors estimated that I had lost about 80 percent of the strength in my left arm. Three fingers on my left hand completely lost feeling. The slightest

movements would send pain waves hurtling down my left side and shoulder. I had to step away completely from my work and wear a neck brace twenty-four hours a day for five weeks.

About halfway through that experience, I was sitting on the screened-in porch behind our home. The day was cold and blustery, but I needed a change of scenery. Suddenly a bird landed on the railing and began to sing. On that cold, rainy day, I couldn't believe any creature had a reason to sing. I wanted to shoot that bird! But he continued to warble, and I had no choice but to listen.

The next day I was on the porch again, but this time it was bright, sunny, and warm. I was tempted to feel sorry for myself when suddenly the bird (at least it looked like the same one) returned. And he was singing again! Where was that shotgun?

Then it hit me: the bird sang in the cold rain as well as the sunny warmth. His song was not altered by outward circumstances, but it was held constant by an internal condition. It was as though God quietly said to me, "You've got the same choice, Bob. You will either let external circumstances mold your attitude, or your attitude will rise above the external circumstances. You choose!"[2]

We have the opportunity to rejoice in hope and be patient through trials. With our hearts and minds focused on our eternal future, we can rejoice in hope despite difficult circumstances. Even through tribulation, we can show God's love by choosing patience. Leon Morris explains that the word patient "denotes not a passive putting up with things, but an active, steadfast endurance." Morris also states that the term tribulation denotes deep and serious trouble.[3]

The third phrase of Romans 12:12 is "constant in prayer." A consistent prayer life gives us the strength to rejoice in hope and find patience when afflicted. John Butler writes:

> For prayer to be effective, it has to be persistent. If the answer does not come in twenty-four hours, many quit praying, which is why so many do not have much success in their prayer life. Persistency in prayer is a mark of true faith.[4]

As you live out true faith, never lose hope. Instead, "Rejoice in hope, be patient in tribulation, be constant in prayer."

Questions:

1. The word "rejoice" found in Romans 12:12 comes from a Greek word that means "to find delight in." In what ways do you find delight in the hope you have in Jesus Christ?

2. How does "rejoicing in hope" help you to "be patient in tribulation"?

3. How does a persistent prayer life strengthen your hope and help you to choose to rejoice?

Day Thirty

Hope

Plentiful Redemption

The cost of redemption cannot be overstated.
The wonders of grace cannot be overemphasized.
Randy Alcorn[1]

The heart of the Gospel is redemption, and the essence of
redemption is the substitutionary sacrifice of Christ.
Charles Spurgeon[2]

Text: Psalm 130:7
[7] O Israel, hope in the Lord! For with the Lord there is steadfast
love, and with him is plentiful redemption.

Thoughts:
Redemption is a key theme found throughout the New
Testament. Biblical redemption is purchasing the rescue or
recovery of a person. Specifically, redemption means setting
someone free by paying a price. It is associated with the terms
ransom and deliverance. Theologically, redemption refers to
Jesus' death on the cross. When our sinless Savior died, He
paid the penalty for our sins. He took the place we deserved
and paid the price none of us could afford to purchase our salvation. What we had all lost because of sin, Jesus bought back
through His final sacrifice on the cross. Jesus rescued through
redemption.

Redemption was a key theme in the Old Testament, powerfully pictured before the cross. The nation of Israel was founded on the principle of redemption. God redeemed Israel from bondage in Egypt. He then gave them the Passover to remember their redemption and celebrate His deliverance.

Psalm 130 is a Song of Ascent. The Songs of Ascents are a group of fifteen psalms from Psalm 120-134 sung by God's people as they journeyed to Jerusalem to attend reminders such as Passover. These psalms are extremely helpful for our spiritual journey because they are powerful reminders of God's redemptive power. The Songs of Ascent can help us find hope amid the trials of this life.

In Psalm 130, the psalmist calls out to God from the depths of despair, desperately hoping God will hear.

Psalm 130:1-2 (ESV)

¹ Out of the depths I cry to you, O Lord! ² O Lord, hear my voice! Let your ears be attentive to the voice of my pleas for mercy!

The psalmist then expresses his hope in God's Word. It is this hope that gives him strength to wait in the Lord.

Psalm 130:5-6 (ESV)

⁵ I wait for the Lord, my soul waits, and in his word I hope; ⁶ my soul waits for the Lord more than watchmen for the morning, more than watchmen for the morning.

Now, we come to our verse for today's devotion.

Psalm 130:7 (ESV)

⁷ O Israel, hope in the Lord! For with the Lord there is steadfast love, and with him is plentiful redemption.

The psalmist had a rich spiritual heritage to draw hope from. He knew that there is steadfast love found in a relationship with the Lord. This hope in the past brought him spiritual renewal in the present.

The psalmist then turns his focus to God's redemption. He says that "with Him is plentiful redemption." As if one redemption wasn't enough, God's redemption is plentiful. "Plentiful" is the Hebrew word *rabah* found 230 times in the Old Testament. This word can mean "to become many, numerous, to make large, to become great, and to bring in abundance." John Phillips writes:

> The expression "plenteous redemption" reminds God's people that He has a thousand ways to rescue those who put their trust in Him. His patience and mercy had not been exhausted by the nation's long and persistent rebellion. Confession and contrition would soon open the floodgates of His lovingkindness.[3]

Israel had witnessed God's redemption on multiple occasions. Every time it seemed hopeless, God rescued them and set them free. God gave His people "plentiful redemption." He rescued them from slavery, gave them multiple victories over their enemies, and brought them to the land He had promised them.

In Psalm 130, the psalmist hoped for a future redemption for God's people. He knew that God brings His redemption in abundance.

As God's children, we can place that same hope in God because He has "plentiful redemption." So, make Psalm 130 personal to you today: "O (believer), hope in the Lord! For with the Lord there is steadfast love, and with him is plentiful redemption."

Questions:

1. How does God's steadfast love connect to His plentiful redemption?

2. How can the abundance of God's redemption renew your hope in Him today?

3. Read Psalm 130:1-8. Imagine singing these words as you journeyed to Jerusalem to celebrate the memory of all that God has done. Write down everything in this Psalm that gives you hope today in Jesus.

Day Thirty-One

Hope

Hope of Righteousness

Christianity doesn't offer a smooth flight; it provides a safe
landing. The promise of Jesus is not one of happiness,
He promises righteousness.
Ray Comfort[1]

Text: Galatians 5:5-6
[5] For through the Spirit, by faith, we ourselves eagerly wait for
the hope of righteousness. [6] For in Christ Jesus neither circumcision nor uncircumcision counts for anything, but only faith
working through love.

Thoughts:
In Galatians 5, Paul is writing to believers who are being
misled by those who taught that an outward sign (circumcision) was required for salvation. Membership in God's Kingdom
is not something earned by our good works or any outward
observances. Salvation is a gift given by Christ and accessed
through faith.

This is what led Paul to write, "For in Christ neither circumcision nor uncircumcision counts for anything, but only
faith working through love" (Galatians 5:6). Our entire Christian life revolves around our position in Christ. Our right
standing before God can never be obtained through religious
observances such as circumcision. Our relationship with Him

comes through the Spirit and not the flesh.

It is only "through the Spirit" and "by faith" that we can receive God's gift of salvation (Galatians 5:5). The Holy Spirit directs our hearts toward the hope of righteousness. There are two approaches to salvation: one is biblical, and the other is worldly. One is human, and the other divine. One leads to salvation, and the other leads to frustration.

The wrong approach to salvation is legalism. Legalism places all hope in the power of self. The problem with legalism is no amount of outward good works can lead to a right standing before God.

The right and only hopeful approach to salvation is through the divine side. God sent His Son to pay the penalty for our sins. God offers us salvation by His grace based on the finished work of Jesus Christ. So, the stark difference between legalism and grace is that one depends on God, and the other on self. In other words, grace depends on God's work while legalism depends on yours.

Where are you going to place your hope for righteousness? Are you really going to place your hope in your current efforts rather than the finished work of Jesus Christ?

Paul found his hope only through Jesus Christ. This led him to write, "We ourselves eagerly wait for the hope of righteousness" (Galatians 5:5). The phrase "we eagerly wait" is found only eight times in the New Testament. It is the Greek word *apekdexomai*. This is an incredible triple compound word, which means it comes from three different New Testament words joined together.

To better understand Paul's statement, let's briefly study the depth of this word. The three words and their respective meanings are as follows: *apo*, "away from," *dexomai*, "welcome," and *ekdikesis*, "out of ". The main root word is the middle word *dexomai*, which carries the idea "to receive through a welcome, to accept by taking into one's own hands." The prefix *apo* intensifies the root word to emphasize separation. Therefore, *apekdexomai* describes looking completely away from this world and focusing on what comes out of being welcomed by God's own hands.

This same triple compound word is noted in the following Scriptures:

Romans 8:23 (ESV)

23 And not only the creation, but we ourselves, who have the firstfruits of the Spirit, groan inwardly as we **wait eagerly** for adoption as sons, the redemption of our bodies.

Hebrews 9:27-28 (ESV)

27 And just as it is appointed for man to die once, and after that comes judgment, 28 so Christ, having been offered once to bear the sins of many, will appear a second time, not to deal with sin but to save those who are **eagerly waiting** for him.

Philippians 3:20-21 (ESV)

20 But our citizenship is in heaven, and from it we **await** a Savior, the Lord Jesus Christ,21 who will transform our lowly body to be like his glorious body, by the power that enables him even to subject all things to himself.

Paul is "eagerly waiting" for what he will receive from God. He hopes for righteousness. Paul knows that when Jesus calls us home to Heaven, God will transform us into complete righteousness. He will complete our salvation by exchanging our fleshy bodies for glorified ones. Then, and only then, will we be made completely righteous for all eternity. As believers, we have much to look forward to! We have a certain hope for future righteousness based on the work of Jesus Christ, our Savior.

Questions:

1. Why is the key to what you receive as a child of God found in Paul's words, "through the Spirit, by faith, . . ."?

2. How does today's study encourage you to "eagerly wait"?

3. What are your thoughts on "the hope of righteousness"?

Day Thirty-Two

Hope

Hope Set on The Living God

I can tell you that God is alive
because I talked to Him this morning!
Billy Graham[1]

Text: 1 Timothy 4:7-10

[7] Have nothing to do with irreverent, silly myths. Rather train yourself for godliness; [8] for while bodily training is of some value, godliness is of value in every way, as it holds promise for the present life and also for the life to come. [9] The saying is trustworthy and deserving of full acceptance. [10] For to this end we toil and strive, because we have our hope set on the living God, who is the Savior of all people, especially of those who believe.

Thoughts:

Paul wrote 1 Timothy to mentor Timothy and instruct him on issues facing the church at Ephesus. The main cause for the letter was to teach Timothy how to lead in ministry while also urging him to resist false teachings.

Rather than listening to "silly myths," Paul told Timothy to "train yourself for godliness." Bryan Chapell and R. Kent Hughes explain Paul's words as follows:

The call to "train yourself to be godly" is highly expressive. The word *train* is a translation of the Greek word *gumnos*, which means "naked" and is the word from which we derive the English word *gymnasium*. In traditional Greek athletic contests, the participants competed without clothing, so their movements would not be hindered. So the word *train* originally carried the literal meaning, "to exercise naked." By New Testament times it referred to exercise and training in general. But even then, it was, and still is, a word with the smell of the gym in it—the sweat of a good workout. "Exercise, work out, train yourself for the purpose of godliness" conveys the feel of what Paul is saying. Run until your feet are like lead, and then choose to sprint. Pump iron until your muscles burn, until another rep is impossible, then do more.

This call comes to us all, and we can see its wisdom throughout all of life. The discipline of training for 10,000 hours enables some of us mortals to run 100 meters in 10 seconds. Hours of watching game films can free a defensive back to play with utter abandon.

But when it comes to spiritual matters, we hesitate. *Discipline* sounds so much like legalism. But such thinking is mistaken. Legalism is self-centered, but discipline is God-centered. The legalistic heart says, "I will do this thing to gain merit with God." The disciplined heart says, "I will do this thing because I love God and want to please Him." Paul knew this difference well, and he never gave an inch to legalists, even while challenging Christians to "train yourself to be godly."[2]

Godly living demands the strenuous striving for goals as found among athletes at the highest level. However, spiritual training towards godliness serves a much higher purpose. Paul expresses that bodily training has some value, but godliness has value "in every way" because it "holds promise for the present life and the life to come" (1 Timothy 4:8).

Robert H. Mounce shares this insight:

> Godliness is valuable because it makes the present life a more abundant life (see John 10:10) and it guarantees continuous fellowship with Christ in the age to come.[3]

The authors of *Exalting Jesus in 1 & 2 Timothy and Titus* add:

> Train in prayer, in the Word, in fasting, in worship, and in sharing the gospel. Spend your time in that kind of training. Your body will only last for a few years, but the gains from godliness will endure forever.[4]

This leads Paul to an incredible conclusion: "For to this end we toil and strive, because we have our hope set on the living God, who is the Savior of all people, especially of those who believe" (1 Timothy 4:10). The end we strive for is godliness. The reason we toil is because our hope is set on the living God. Notice that our hope is "set." This is not an isolated act of hope that occurs occasionally. This is a continuous attitude of hope that is established in our hearts.

Our hope is in the living God. Jesus is alive and well. He is victorious over death and seated at the right hand of the Father. He is "The Savior of all people, especially of those who believe" (1 Timothy 4:10). Christ saves every person who puts his or her faith in Him.

So exercise spiritually for godliness. Train for what makes a difference now and for all eternity. And remember, a huge part of what keeps you in spiritual shape is the hope you exercise daily in your living God.

Questions:
1. In what ways do people focus more on physical exercise than their spiritual training?

2. What does your dedication to spiritual training say about the amount of hope you've placed in Christ?

3. In what specific ways is your hope set on the living God?

Day Thirty-Three

Hope

Surely There Is a Future

[13] My son, eat honey, for it is good, and the
drippings of the honeycomb are sweet to your taste.
[14] Know that wisdom is such to your soul;
if you find it, there will be a future,
and your hope will not be cut off.
Proverbs 24:13-14 (ESV)

Text: Proverbs 23:17-18
[17] Let not your heart envy sinners, but continue in the fear of
the Lord all the day. [18] Surely there is a future, and your hope
will not be cut off.

Thoughts:
   In total, five books of the Bible are categorized as Wisdom
Literature: Job, Psalms, Proverbs, Ecclesiastes, and Song of Solomon. Dennis Bratcher provides a concise description of Wisdom Literature:

   Wisdom is an approach to life, a way of looking
   at the world, and for Israelites, a way of living out in
   very deliberate, rational ways their commitment to
   God. While wisdom's roots go back to the early days
   of Israelite history, it began to flower in the latter
   part of the Old Testament period and flourished in

131

the Intertestamental period and the era of the New Testament (400 BC to AD 100).

Here are two brief characteristics of Old Testament Wisdom perspectives: Israelite Wisdom is rooted in reverence and commitment to God. Wisdom is concerned with how to live well in everyday life.[1]

Therefore, Proverbs give practical instructions for wise living.

In Proverbs 23:17-18, the proverb writer instructs the reader not to envy sinners. If we are not careful, we might look at the earthly possessions of wicked people and question why their sins seem to go unpunished while their unrighteousness appears to be rewarded. It is easy to fall into this trap if we only think about this side of eternity. Yet the ultimate judgment of God is coming and lasts forever.

Proverbs 23:17 teaches us to "continue in the fear of the Lord all the day." Rather than being jealous of sinners, we should live with an eternal focus founded in a reverent fear of the Lord. A holy reverence of God that results from a sacred awe of who He is causes us to live with a constant recognition of His greatness. A true fear of the Lord is always accompanied by a child-like trust that submits to His Lordship and obeys His commands.

The next verse, Proverbs 23:18, gives the reason not to envy sinners and to continually fear the Lord: "Surely there is a future, and your hope will not be cut off." If this earthly life was the only life we lived, we would have much more reason to envy those with a seemingly better life here. But this life is not the only life we live! We are headed from this temporary life to an everlasting one. Since we are sure there is an eternal future with God, we live with great hope. Hope plays a major role in the Christian walk as we anticipate eternity with our Lord.

Jesus Christ is coming back, and we can confidently say that we will dwell with Him forever. John tells us about this message from God in Revelation 22:20: "He who testifies to these things says, 'Surely I am coming soon.' Amen. Come, Lord Jesus!" If Jesus said He is coming, we know there is a future.

Theologian and author Frederick Dale Bruner shares the following story, which perfectly illustrates today's Scripture:

> When Pastor David Peterson was preparing a sermon, his little daughter came in and asked, "Daddy, can we play?"
>
> "I'm sorry, sweetheart, but I'm right in the middle of preparing this sermon. In about an hour, I can play," her dad said.
>
> "OK," she said. "When you're finished, I will give you a great big hug."
>
> She went to the door, then did a U-turn and came back to give her dad a bone-breaking hug.
>
> "You said you were going to give me a hug *after* I finished," her dad said, teasing.
>
> "I just wanted you to know what you have to look forward to!" the little girl said.
>
> God wants us to know, through His first coming, how much we have to look forward to in His second. [2]

Remember that God promises us that our hope will not be cut off. Therefore, as God's children, we have great expectations for a certain future.

Questions:

1. How does a fear of the Lord tie into your future hope?

2. What are your thoughts on these words from Proverbs 23:18: "Surely there is a future."

3. How does it strengthen your hope to know that it will never be cut off?

Day Thirty-Four

Hope

Hope Stored Up for You in Heaven

Hope is patiently waiting expectantly
for the intangible to become reality.
Avery Miller[1]

If you read history, you will find that
the Christians who did most for the present world were
precisely those who thought most of the next.
C. S. Lewis[2]

Text: Colossians 1:3-6a (NIV)
[3] We always thank God, the Father of our Lord Jesus Christ, when we pray for you, [4] because we have heard of your faith in Christ Jesus and of the love you have for all God's people - [5] the faith and love that spring from the hope stored up for you in heaven and about which you have already heard in the true message of the gospel [6] that has come to you.

Thoughts:
The Apostle Paul, writing to the Church at Colossae, mentions again the three greatest virtues of the Christian life. This time Paul mentions them in the following order: faith, love, and hope. J. B. Lightfoot explains these three virtues as follows: "Faith rests on the past; love works in the present; hope looks to the future."[3]

Brian Harbour provides great instruction and application to Paul's words found in Colossians 1:3-5:

> Hope as it is used in this verse is not a subjective feeling but an objective fact.
>
> On a hot summer day in Dallas, someone might say, "I've heard it is going to rain today." We respond, "I hope so." That is hope as a subjective feeling.
>
> That's not the way the word is used in our text. Hope, in this case, is an objective fact. Notice three ideas about our hope reflected in the text.
>
> First, hope produces faith and love. That is the opposite of what we normally think. We think of hope as being produced by our faith. Yet, Paul said in our text that our faith and "love spring from the hope."
>
> Why do we keep believing even when our circumstances are awful? Why do we keep loving even when people shun our love? It is because of our hope in Christ.
>
> Second, our hope is secure. This hope is "stored up for you in heaven." It is not deposited in some bank which might eventually fail. It is not invested in the stock market which might ultimately fall. Our hope is stored up for us in heaven. It is secure.
>
> Third, hope comes from the Gospel. The Colossian Christians received this hope through "the gospel that has come to you." Jesus Christ provides something we can receive from no other source. He provides a relationship with the eternal God which guarantees our future.
>
> That's why the message of Christ is called good news. It gives us security about the future which enables us to make it through the insecurities of the present. Jesus gives us hope. This hope was deeply rooted in the lives of the Colossians.[4]

Our hope is founded on the Gospel and stored up in Heaven. Hope looks ahead. Hope has to do with the future, and what a glorious future it is! Our hope is guaranteed by God Himself in His infallible Word. Put your hope in Christ and in the future resurrection He has in store for His children.

Questions:
1. How does knowing you have hope stored up for you in Heaven increase your hope today?

2. Why do you think Scripture repeatedly connects faith, hope, and love? How does the order of these virtues indicate a deeper truth?

3. How does the following quote give you perspective to never lose hope?

> When you say that a situation or a person is hopeless, you are slamming the door in the face of God.
> **Charles L. Allen**[5]

Day Thirty-Five

Hope

The Helmet of the Hope of Salvation

Hope is never ill when faith is well.
John Bunyan[1]

Text: 1 Thessalonians 5:8-11
⁸ But since we belong to the day, let us be sober, having put on the breastplate of faith and love, and for a helmet the hope of salvation. ⁹ For God has not destined us for wrath, but to obtain salvation through our Lord Jesus Christ,¹⁰ who died for us so that whether we are awake or asleep we might live with him. ¹¹ Therefore encourage one another and build one another up, just as you are doing.

Thoughts:
The theme of 1 Thessalonians is the Second Coming of Jesus Christ, which is called "The Day of the Lord" in chapter 5. Scripture says that Jesus will come like a thief in the night (1 Thessalonians 5:2). Paul states that believers are not in the darkness (1 Thessalonians 5:5) and "belong to the day" (1 Thessalonians 5:8). Since we belong to the day and are children of light, we live prepared for Jesus' Second Coming.

As believers, we are battle-ready awaiting the return of our King. In our Scripture for today, Paul reminds us to put on the breastplate of faith and love and the helmet of the hope of our salvation. So, Christians awaiting Christ put on faith, love, and hope. In faith, we trust in God's promises. With love, we worship God and love our neighbor. This faith displayed with love causes us to live with a constant hope for the future God has in store. These three virtues of faith, love, and hope are essential for the spiritual warfare we face.

A pastor once said:

"When faith is weak, love grows cold. When love grows cold, hope is lost. When hope in God's promise of future glory is weak, believers are vulnerable to temptation and sin."[2]

Therefore, every believer must possess these three virtues to find victory over the enemy.

The statement in 1 Thessalonians 5:8 reminds us of what Paul wrote to the Church at Ephesus:

Ephesians 6:13-17 (ESV)
[13] Therefore take up the whole armor of God, that you may be able to withstand in the evil day, and having done all, to stand firm. [14] Stand therefore, having fastened on the belt of truth, and having put on the breastplate of righteousness, [15] and, as shoes for your feet, having put on the readiness given by the gospel of peace. [16] In all circumstances take up the shield of faith, with which you can extinguish all the flaming darts of the evil one; [17] and take the helmet of salvation, and the sword of the Spirit, which is the word of God.

Notice that the last two pieces of armor that Paul mentions are the helmet and sword. This makes perfect sense as you are getting dressed for battle. If you put on your helmet first, you couldn't see to put on your shoes. With clear vision, we get dressed for battle. Then the last two items that get us battle-ready are the helmet and the sword.

The helmet is the sure knowledge of your salvation. The helmet of salvation guards our thoughts and gives us peace amid chaos. Knowing that you are a saved child of God, gives you complete confidence as you face life's battles. It also provides a firm assurance that your future is secure.

The sword of the Spirit is the Word of God. In a battle, communication with your Commander in Chief is critical. God speaks the clearest through His Word. The more you study God's Word, the closer your relationship will be with Him.

With the knowledge of your salvation and the promises from His Word, you always have hope. So live daily with the confident assurance of your salvation. Because you are His child, cherish your daily time in Scripture hearing His voice in every verse. Put on your helmet and pick up your sword. With your salvation and His Word, you never have to lose hope!

Questions:
1. How does being battle-ready for spiritual warfare give you hope?

2. What are some practical ways you can put on your spiritual helmet and pick up your spiritual sword every day?

3. In *Never Lose Hope*, what have you learned to help you live with a confident expectation for the future?

Never Lose Hope

Notes

Contents

[1]Crotts, John. 2021. *Hope: Living Confidently in God*. Edited by Deepak Reju. 31-Day Devotionals for Life. Phillipsburg, NJ: P&R Publishing.

[2]Pentz, Croft M. 1990. *The Complete Book of Zingers: Over 5,000 Perfect One-Liners*. Carol Stream, IL: Tyndale House Publishers, Inc.

Introduction

[1]Strobel, Lee. 2015. *The Case for Hope: Looking Ahead with Confidence and Courage*. Grand Rapids, MI: Zondervan.

Day 1

[1]Strobel, Lee. 2015. *The Case for Hope: Looking Ahead with Confidence and Courage*. Grand Rapids, MI: Zondervan.

[2]Ibid.

[3]Boice, James Montgomery. 1991–. *Romans: The New Humanity*. Vol. 4. Grand Rapids, MI: Baker Book House.

Day 2

[1]MacDonald, J. (n.d.). *Top 19 God promises quotes: AZ quotes*. azquotes.com. https://www.azquotes.com/quotes/topics/god-promises.html

[2]Lucado, Max. 2018. *Unshakable Hope: Building Our Lives on the Promises of God*. New York, NY: Thomas Nelson.

Day 3
[1]Rhodes, Ron. 2011. *1001 Unforgettable Quotes about God, Faith, & the Bible*. Eugene, OR: Harvest House Publishers.
[2]Phillips, John. 2012. *Exploring Psalms 89–150: An Expository Commentary*. Vol. 2. The John Phillips Commentary Series. Kregel Publications; WORDsearch Corp.

Day 4
[1]Prichard, S. (2023, May 26). *Quotes on hope*. Skip Prichard | Leadership Insights. https://www.skipprichard.com/quotes-on-hope/

Day 5
[1]Shepherd, V. (2021, May 14). *Hope*. Grace Quotes. https://gracequotes.org/topic/hope/
[2]Coekin, Richard. 2015. *Ephesians for You*. Edited by Carl Laferton. God's Word for You. The Good Book Company.
[3]Ibid.

Day 6
[1]Goff, B. (2016, October 25). *God hasn't brought you this far*. SermonQuotes. https://sermonquotes.com/authors/9432-god-hasnt-brought-far.html
[2]Swindoll, Charles R. 2016. *The Tale of the Tardy Oxcart and 1501 Other Stories*. Nashville, TN: Thomas Nelson.
[3] Jeremiah, David. 2021. Hope: Living Fearlessly in a Scary World. Tyndale House Publishers, Inc.
[4]Dunnam, Maxie D., and Lloyd J. Ogilvie. 1982. *Galatians / Ephesians / Philippians / Colossians / Philemon*. Vol. 31. The Preacher's Commentary Series. Nashville, TN: Thomas Nelson Inc.

Day 7

[1]Munson, J. (2023, May 10). *The god who delights - right from the heart ministries*. Right From The Heart Ministries - Sharing the love of Jesus through media. https://rightfromtheheart.org/devotions/the-god-who-delights/

[2]Ryle, J. C. (2021, May 14). *Hope*. Grace Quotes. https://gracequotes.org/topic/hope/

Day 8

[1]Butler, John G. 2010. *Analytical Bible Expositor: 1 & 2 Peter*. Clinton, IA: LBC Publications.

Day 9

[1]Crotts, John. 2021. *Hope: Living Confidently in God*. Edited by Deepak Reju. 31-Day Devotionals for Life. Phillipsburg, NJ: P&R Publishing.

[2]Mohler, R. Albert, Jr. 2017. *Exalting Jesus in Hebrews*. Nashville, TN: Holman Reference.

Day 10

[1]F. F. Bruce, *1 and 2 Thessalonians,* Word Biblical Commentary (Waco, Texas: Word Books, Publisher, 1982), p. 196.

Day 11

[1]Wright, Tom. 2004. *Hebrews for Everyone*. London: Society for Promoting Christian Knowledge.

[2]Ibid.

[3]Piper, J. (2024, May 4). *What's the difference between faith and hope?* Desiring God. https://www.desiringgod.org/interviews/whats-the-difference-between-faith-and-hope

Day 12
[1]Jeremiah, David. 2021. Hope: Living Fearlessly in a Scary World. Tyndale House Publishers, Inc.
[2]Ibid.

Day 13
[1]Hughes, R. Kent. 1991. *Romans: Righteousness from Heaven*. Preaching the Word. Wheaton, IL: Crossway Books.
[2]Larson, Craig Brian. 2002. *750 Engaging Illustrations for Preachers, Teachers & Writers*. Grand Rapids, MI: Baker Books.

Day 14
[1]Young, S. (n.d.). *A quote from Jesus Calling.* Goodreads. https://www.goodreads.com/quotes/5335399
[2]Moore, B. (2021, September 10). *25 quotes to give you hope*. Crosswalk.com. https://www.crosswalk.com/faith/spiritual-life/inspiring-quotes/25-quotes-to-give-you-hope.html

Day 15
[1]Chesterton, G. K. (n.d.). *53 Christian quotes on hope including Bible verses*. The Powerful Victory Mind. http://victoryminded.com/53-christian-quotes-on-hope-including-bible-verses/
[2]Wilson, William. 1987. *New Wilson's Old Testament Word Studies: Keyed to Strong's Numbering System and to Theological Wordbook of the Old Testament*. Grand Rapids, Mich.: Kregel Publications.
[3]Strong, James, John R Kohlenberger, and James A Swanson. 2001. *The Strongest Strong's Exhaustive Concordance of the Bible*. Grand Rapids, Mich.: Zondervan.

Day 16

[1]Publishing, Barbour, Inc. 2011. *The Complete Guide to Christian Quotations: An Indispensable Resource for Writers, Pastors, Teachers, Students--and Anyone Else Who Loves Books*. Uhrichsville, OH: Barbour Books.

[2]Butler, John G. 2009. *Analytical Bible Expositor: I & II Corinthians*. Clinton, IA: LBC Publications.

Day 17

[1]Publishing, Barbour, Inc. 2011. *The Complete Guide to Christian Quotations: An Indispensable Resource for Writers, Pastors, Teachers, Students--and Anyone Else Who Loves Books*. Uhrichsville, OH: Barbour Books.

[2]Naselli, Andrew David. (2022, August 16). *Why Romans is the greatest letter ever written*. Crossway. https://www.crossway.org/articles/why-romans-is-the-greatest-letter-ever-written/

[3]Keller, Timothy. 2014. *Romans 1–7 for You*. Edited by Carl Laferton. God's Word for You. The Good Book Company.

[4]Ibid.

[5]Tripp, Paul David. (2020, August 15). *4 reasons for hope in suffering*. Crossway. https://www.crossway.org/articles/4-reasons-for-hope-in-suffering/

Day 18

[1]Frazer, S. (2021, March 18). *Even in the dark: Finding hope in christ in every season*. Well. https://wellwateredwomen.com/even-in-the-dark/

[2]Larson, Craig Brian, and Phyllis Ten Elshof. 2008. *1001 Illustrations That Connect*. Grand Rapids, MI: Zondervan Publishing House.

[3]Piper, J. (2023, December 19). *Subjected to futility in hope, part 1*. Desiring God. https://www.desiringgod.org/messages/subjected-to-futility-in-hope-part-1

Day 19

[1]TerKeurst, L. (n.d.). *Top 25 God is with you quotes: A-Z quotes*. https://www.azquotes.com/quotes/topics/god-is-with-you.html
[2]Wilson, Jim L., and Rodger Russell. 2015. "Trapped in His Body for 23 Years." In *300 Illustrations for Preachers*, edited by Elliot Ritzema. Bellingham, WA: Lexham Press.

Day 20

[1]Guzik, David. 2013. *Romans*. David Guzik's Commentaries on the Bible. Santa Barbara, CA: David Guzik.
[2]Runge, Steven E. 2014. *High Definition Commentary: Romans*. Bellingham, WA: Lexham Press.
[3]Guzik, David. 2013. *Romans*. David Guzik's Commentaries on the Bible. Santa Barbara, CA: David Guzik.
[4]Runge, Steven E. 2014. *High Definition Commentary: Romans*. Bellingham, WA: Lexham Press.

Day 21

[1]Tozer, A. W. (n.d.). *A quote by A.W. Tozer*. Goodreads. https://www.goodreads.com/quotes/376518-what-comes-into-our-minds-when-we-think-about-god

Day 22

[1]Larson, Craig Brian, and Phyllis Ten Elshof. 2008. *1001 Illustrations That Connect*. Grand Rapids, MI: Zondervan Publishing House.

Day 23

[1]Augustine. (2015, April 3). *Jesus Christ-humanity*. Grace Quotes. https://gracequotes.org/topic/jesus_christ-humanity/

Day 24

[1]Tozer, A. W. (n.d.-b). *God's presence quotes (50 quotes)*. Goodreads. https://www.goodreads.com/quotes/tag/god-s-presence#

Day 25

[1]Dyke, H. V. (n.d.). *Top 13 Jesus birth quotes: A-Z quotes.* https://www.azquotes.com/quotes/topics/jesus-birth.html
[2]Larson, Craig Brian, and Phyllis Ten Elshof. 2008. *1001 Illustrations That Connect.* Grand Rapids, MI: Zondervan Publishing House.
[3]Lewis, C. S. 2017. *Mere Christianity.* Harpercollins Publishers. (Orig. pub. 1952.).

Day 26

[1]Barton, Bruce B., David Veerman, Linda Chaffee Taylor, and Grant R. Osborne. 1997. *Luke.* Life Application Bible Commentary. Wheaton, IL: Tyndale House Publishers.
[2]Ibid.

Day 27

[1] Packer, J. I. (n.d.). *Top 25 Christian hope quotes: A-Z quotes.* azquotes.com. https://www.azquotes.com/quotes/topics/christian-hope.html
[2]Phillips, John. 2009. *Exploring the Gospel of John: An Expository Commentary.* The John Phillips Commentary Series. Kregel Publications; WORDsearch Corp.
[3]Swartley, Willard M. 2013. *Believers Church Bible Commentary: John.* Edited by Douglas B. Miller and Loren L. Johns. Harrisonburg, VA; Waterloo, ON: Herald Press.

Day 28

[1]Dunnam, Maxie D., and Lloyd J. Ogilvie. 1982. *Galatians / Ephesians / Philippians / Colossians / Philemon.* Vol. 31. The Preacher's Commentary Series. Nashville, TN: Thomas Nelson Inc.
[2]Cole, Steven J. 2017. "Lesson 7: Serving Christ Well (Colossians 1:24–27)." In *Colossians,* Col 1:26–27. Steven J. Cole Commentary Series. Dallas: Galaxie Software.

[3]Wright, N. T. 1986. *Colossians and Philemon: An Introduction and Commentary*. Vol. 12. Tyndale New Testament Commentaries. Downers Grove, IL: InterVarsity Press.

Day 29
[1]Rhodes, Ron. 2011. *1001 Unforgettable Quotes about God, Faith, & the Bible*. Eugene, OR: Harvest House Publishers.
[2]Larson, Craig Brian, and Phyllis Ten Elshof. 2008. *1001 Illustrations That Connect*. Grand Rapids, MI: Zondervan Publishing House.
[3]Guzik, David. 2013. *Romans*. David Guzik's Commentaries on the Bible. Santa Barbara, CA: David Guzik.
[4]Butler, John G. 2009. *Analytical Bible Expositor: Romans*. Clinton, IA: LBC Publications.

Day 30
[1]Alcorn, R. (2023, September 20). *Sermon quotes on redemption*. The Pastor's Workshop. https://thepastorsworkshop.com/sermon-quotes-on-redemption/
[2]Spurgeon, C. (2023, September 20). *Sermon quotes on redemption*. The Pastor's Workshop. https://thepastorsworkshop.com/sermon-quotes-on-redemption/
[3]Phillips, John. 2012. *Exploring Psalms 89–150: An Expository Commentary*. Vol. 2. The John Phillips Commentary Series. Kregel Publications; WORDsearch Corp.

Day 31
[1]Comfort, R. (n.d.). *Top 25 righteousness quotes (of 718): A-Z quotes*. https://www.azquotes.com/quotes/topics/righteousness.html

Day 32
[1]Graham, B. (n.d.). *Top 500 Billy Graham Quotes (2024 update)*. Quotefancy. https://quotefancy.com/billy-graham-quotes
[2]Hughes, R. K., & Chapell, B. (2000). *1 & 2 Timothy and Titus: To Guard the Deposit* (p. 108). Wheaton, IL: Crossway Books.

[3]Mounce, Robert H. 2005. *Pass It On: A Bible Commentary for Laymen: First and Second Timothy*. Eugene, OR: Wipf & Stock Publishers.
[4]Akin, D. L., and Merida, T. (2013). *Exalting Jesus in 1 & 2 Timothy and Titus* (1 Ti 4:1–16). Nashville, TN: Holman Reference.

Day 33
[1]Bratcher, D. (n.d.). *The Character of Wisdom: An Introduction to Old Testament Wisdom Literature*. http://www.crivoice.org/wisdom.html
[2]Larson, Craig Brian, and Phyllis Ten Elshof. 2008. *1001 Illustrations That Connect*. Grand Rapids, MI: Zondervan Publishing House.

Day 34
[1]Miller, A. (2024, April 26). *You searched for hope*. Daily Christian Quotes. https://www.dailychristianquote.com/?s=Hope
[2]Morgan, Robert J. 2000. *Nelson's Complete Book of Stories, Illustrations, and Quotes*. Electronic ed. Nashville: Thomas Nelson Publishers.
[3]Lightfoot, Joseph Barber. 1886. *Saint Paul's Epistles to the Colossians and to Philemon*. 8th ed. Classic Commentaries on the Greek New Testament. London; New York: Macmillan and Co.
[4]Harbour, Brian L. 2013. "Notable Harbour Verse Studies." In *Verse by Verse Bible Studies on Colossians*, Col 1:5. WORDsearch.
[5]Allen, C. (2024, April 26). *You searched for hope*. Daily Christian Quotes. https://www.dailychristianquote.com/?s=Hope

Day 35
[1]Rhodes, Ron. 2011. *1001 Unforgettable Quotes about God, Faith, & the Bible*. Eugene, OR: Harvest House Publishers.
[2]Cole, Steven J. 2017. "Lesson 15: Are You Ready for That Day? (1 Thessalonians 5:1–8)." In *1 Thessalonians*, 1 Th 5:1–8. Steven J. Cole Commentary Series. Dallas: Galaxie Software.

Made in the USA
Columbia, SC
22 October 2024

44860793R00089